Praying for the
Prophetic
Destiny *of the*
UNITED STATES AND
THE PRESIDENCY OF
Donald J. Trump
FROM THE COURTS OF HEAVEN

DESTINY IMAGE BOOKS BY ROBERT HENDERSON

Father, Friend, and Judge

*Prayers and Declarations that Open
the Courts of Heaven*

Operating in the Courts of Heaven

*Receiving Healing from the Courts of Heaven Unlocking Destinies
from the Courts of Heaven Accessing the Courts of Heaven*

The Cloud of Witnesses in the Courts of Heaven

The Books of Heaven

Praying for the
Prophetic Destiny *of the*

UNITED STATES AND
THE PRESIDENCY OF
Donald J. Trump

FROM THE COURTS OF HEAVEN

ROBERT
HENDERSON

DESTINY IMAGE® PUBLISHERS, INC.
P.O. Box 310, Shippensburg, PA 17257-0310
"Promoting Inspired Lives."

This book and all other Destiny Image and Destiny Image Fiction books are available at Christian bookstores and distributors worldwide.

Cover design by Eileen Rockwell

For more information on foreign distributors, call 717-532-3040.

Reach us on the Internet: www.destinyimage.com.

ISBN 13 TP: 978-0-7684-5361-4

ISBN HC: 978-0-7684-5444-4

ISBN 13 eBook: 978-0-7684-5362-1

For Worldwide Distribution, Printed in the U.S.A.

2 3 4 5 6 7 8 / 23 22 21 20

CONTENTS

Chapter 1   The Assignment 7

Chapter 2   Dream Number 1: Shifting the Election. 15

Chapter 3   Standing in the Counsel of the Lord 27

Chapter 4   All Flesh Is as Grass. 37

Chapter 5   Dream Number 2: Seated in the Cabinet. 49

Chapter 6   Four Levels of Judgement 61

Chapter 7   Dream Number 3: Running Mate 71

Chapter 8   Behold Their Threatenings. 81

Chapter 9   Partnering with God 91

Chapter 10   Books of Remembrance. 103

Chapter 11   A Cry for Mercy 115

Chapter 1

THE
ASSIGNMENT

I grew up in an era when love for God and love of country were almost synonymous. In grade school every morning, three things happened over the intercom system of our public school. First, "The Star-Spangled Banner" was played. We each stood at our desks with our hands over our hearts in honor of our country. We listened and sang the lyrics of this song with admiration for the country we lived in.

Oh, say can you see by the dawn's early light

What so proudly we hailed
at the twilight's last gleaming?

Whose broad stripes and bright stars
through the perilous fight,

O'er the ramparts we watched
were so gallantly streaming?

And the rocket's red glare,
the bombs bursting in air,

Gave proof through the night that
our flag was still there.

Oh, say does that star-spangled banner yet wave
O'er the land of the free and
the home of the brave?

As students, each one of us was familiar with the story behind this song.

The lyrics come from the "Defence of Fort M'Henry," a poem written on September 14,

> 1814, by the then 35-year-old lawyer and amateur
> poet Francis Scott Key after witnessing the
> bombardment of Fort McHenry by British ships
> of the Royal Navy in Baltimore Harbor during
> the Battle of Baltimore in the War of 1812.
> Key was inspired by the large U.S. flag, with 15
> stars and 15 stripes, known as the Star-Spangled
> Banner, flying triumphantly above the fort during
> the U.S. victory (from Wikipedia).

This birthed in us an awareness of what our flag stood for and the need to honor the nation it represented.

The next thing we did each morning after singing "The Star-Spangled Banner" as our national anthem was we recited the Pledge of Allegiance to our flag. While we still stood and faced the flag in our room with our hands again over our hearts, we spoke these words:

> I pledge allegiance to the flag of the United States
> of America, and to the republic for which it
> stands, one nation under God, indivisible, with
> liberty and justice for all.

We were taught that our nation and the flag that represented it was of utmost importance and we should be proud to be Americans. This was bred into us as children. After these two things were done, every morning there was then a devotional read and a prayer offered *in Jesus' Name*. This was in a public school. Even after the horrendous ruling of the Supreme Court in 1963 that outlawed prayer in school, there was still this standard of operation in our school. This cultivated a love of country and God in my heart.

My wife Mary, on the other hand, was raised in a military family. She tells that when they were living on Air Force bases around the world, if "The Star-Spangled Banner" was played they had to stop immediately, stand still, and place their hands over their hearts wherever they were, no matter what they were doing. This was done even if they were on the playground or involved in other activities. For some this would seem extreme. Yet this was all designed to foster in the hearts of us as American citizens a love for our nation and a devotion to its values. This was not a burden but was something that birthed great pride and confidence in us as Americans and in our country.

The other time of intense patriotism etched on my mind and heart was when our oldest son graduated from the naval base in Great Lakes, Michigan. He had enlisted in the Navy and had gone to boot camp there. Mary and I went to his graduation and the ceremony associated with it. I will never forget hearing the sound of this marching group long before I could see them. All these sailors, having completed this time of training with a pride and patriotism instilled in their hearts, came marching and chanting and singing "Anchors Aweigh" with the U.S. flag flying and other "colors" representing the Navy. It was an awesome presentation that caused great love of country to emerge again in my heart as I sat as a spectator of this display. There was a mixture of love of nation, appreciation to God for allowing me to be a part of this nation, and a spirit that would have died to defend its values and purpose.

I know some would disagree, but because America was birthed out of a covenant with God by our forefathers, I believe a love for country and a love for God and His purposes are intertwined when it comes to the United States. That doesn't mean that everything in the U.S. is what God would desire. Neither does it mean even our founding fathers had everything right or according to God's purpose. It does, however, mean that the hand of God is on America and the Lord has had and still has a plan for our nation and country. The problem is that the desire of God for our nation has been methodically hijacked. In other words, there has been a thought-out satanic plan to steal away the destiny of America and replace it with one driven by the anti-Christ spirit. Make no mistake. This has not happened by accident but with a diabolical scheme whose origin is from hell. God, however, does not let His purpose in a nation go that easily. In First Samuel 3:1-4 we see God raising up a prophetic voice to reclaim His purposes in a nation.

> *Now the boy Samuel ministered to the Lord before Eli. And the word of the Lord was rare in those days; there was no widespread revelation. And it came to pass at that time, while Eli was lying down in his place, and when his eyes had begun to grow so dim that he could not see, and before the lamp of God went out in the tabernacle of the Lord where the ark of God was, and while Samuel was lying down, that the Lord called Samuel. And he answered, "Here I am!"*

Notice that *before the lamp of God went out*, God called and commissioned Samuel to speak for Him. This tells us that God was not going to allow the light of who He was and His purpose in Israel to be extinguished so easily. He was going to raise up a voice to ignite again His purposes in a nation. I believe the same thing is happening in America today. A nation that many would claim God is finished with because of our rebellion against Him,

God is *reclaiming* for Himself. This is why Donald J. Trump was *miraculously* elected President of the United States. It was God's statement that He *still* has a plan and purpose in America.

I know many have great difficulty with Donald Trump and his ways of communication and leadership. However, when you look at what he promised during his campaign and what he has delivered, the results speak for themselves. I am amazed at how blind some are to this. During the previous administrations of both Democrat and Republican presidencies, there has been a downward spiral away from what God would desire. We have watched as godlessness has abounded with policies against God being set in place. Everything from liberal judges being positioned, to persecution of Christian values, to a president declaring that we are no longer a *Christian nation* (Obama), to same-sex marriages being legalized and too many other atrocious things to mention. Yet when President Trump makes powerful and dramatic moves to curb this downward spiral it seems that many believers can't appreciate or recognize this. All I can credit this to is there is no connection between what they say they believe and their political stance. They don't get that Christian beliefs must affect every aspect of life, including politics and government.

I lay the blame for this at the model of church we predominantly have in America. It is one that preaches a gospel that has no conviction in it; therefore, we are producing *Christians* who have a belief system that doesn't translate into proper voting booth activity. Instead of being a people willing to sacrifice ourselves for the purposes of God, we have become a people of entitlement who expect to be served. We have lost sight of the statement of John F. Kennedy when he said, "Ask not what your country can do for you; ask what you can do for your country." By the way, he was a Democrat. How far from those days in the 1960s the Democratic party has slipped. We don't value the things God deeply values and esteems. The election of Donald Trump was produced by God in His mercy seeking to turn a nation back to His standards and ways. Just like in Samuel, before the *lamp of God* was completely extinguished and quenched, God moved on behalf of a nation. The Lord doesn't only want to stop the *lamp* of His witness from going out; He desires to breathe upon it and ignite it with new fire and influence. We, however, are in a fight for the soul, purpose, and destiny of God in America.

In the next chapters, we will look at *how* the Lord is moving and *how* we must respond and agree with Him. Otherwise, a nation and its destiny and future designed by God may be lost. I will share three distinct dreams that have been prophetic words to me, but I believe also to the body of Christ in this hour. In these dreams there were assignments given and understanding granted for where we are as a nation and as the body of Christ. We must stand up together and contend for the passion of the Lord in America. His chosen vessel to accomplish this with us in this hour is President Donald J. Trump. I declare, *"Let the church arise and take her stand. Let us contend until the will of God is seen in America and her future is secured."*

Lord, as we stand before Your Courts and the Counsel of the Lord, we ask for a returning of America and the nations to the God-ordained purposes of God. May a passion arise in the hearts of Your people to love their country as You, Lord, have loved it. We ask, Lord, that there will be a repenting and a returning to the values that are in Your heart for our nation. Lord, would You allow a patriotic passion to come again into our hearts that we might be willing to lay our lives down for Your desire in our nation. In Jesus' Name, amen!

Chapter 2

Dream Number 1: Shifting the Election

I N March of 2016, Mary and I were on a ministry trip to Germany. This was during the Republican primary that was being waged with many contending to be the Republican candidate for president of the United States. There were ten to twelve still fighting for the right to run against Hilary Clinton, who would become the Democratic nominee in the November 2016 general election. After a busy schedule of ministry in Esslingen, Germany, Mary and I went to bed. As I slept on this particular night, Donald Trump called me on the phone in my dream. He said to me, *"I need for you to do a conference to shift things concerning the election for me on July 6th."* This was the entire dream. As I awoke the next morning, I said to Mary, *"Donald Trump called me on the phone last night."* As I told her this, she laughed. I kind of thought it was funny too, but I knew something significant was being revealed also. I said, *"No, it's real and I've been given an assignment."* First of all, I knew I was to hold a gathering and recruit people from around the nation for this. I knew I was to function in the conference from a *Court of Heaven* perspective and seek to get things set in the spirit realm for Donald Trump to be president. I will explain this more later.

When Donald Trump announced his intentions of campaigning for President of the United States on June 16, 2015, Mary and I were immediately on board. We both very quickly felt and sensed the hand of God on this endeavor. Even though the media mocked and ridiculed and people who were our friends wanted others to become the Republican nominee, we *knew* it was Donald Trump. We simply had this distinct awareness that God's purpose was in this endeavor. Many and even most of my *prophetic* friends wanted Ted Cruz. I could not go there. Even though I've never claimed to be a prophet nor do I now, I prophetically knew Donald Trump was the one God had chosen. When I had this dream ten months later, it therefore wasn't hard for me to process. I already felt strongly he was the guy, so to have him *call me* was not that far out of the box in thought or rationale. From the dream, though, I knew that I was being given an assignment to be a part of the process of seeing Donald Trump elected. I also knew the revelation I carry concerning the Courts of Heaven was a key and critical point. Let me take a moment and explain the Court of Heaven and its importance in the process of Donald Trump's election.

I personally believe that the Court of Heaven message is the X-factor or missing ingredient that has been lacking in the body of Christ and our ability to see cultural change. In my humble opinion it would seem that all our spiritual warfare without the Court of Heaven understanding has produced little on a national level. From the time that *spiritual warfare* began to be emphasized in the mid-1990s, our nation and the policies governing it consistently went the wrong direction. In spite of all our praying, declaring, decreeing and other spiritual efforts, we saw abortion still rampant, gay rights advance, same-sex marriages enacted, wrong judges set in place in the Supreme Court and other federal benches, men being allowed in women's restrooms, and all sorts of other godless idiocies. All the while, the church was making our decrees, yelling at demons, binding powers of darkness, and other supposed spiritual gyrations. Yet clearly we were losing ground in what appeared to be ever-increasing dimensions.

Then the Court of Heaven began to be understood. We saw that attacking powers of darkness that claim a legal right to influence a nation without revoking those legal rights *first* is not effective. In fact, if you attack them while they still maintain a judicial privilege, it can empower them and their activity against us. We see this principle in Revelation 19:11 where Jesus' manner of conflict is revealed.

> *Now I saw heaven opened, and behold, a white horse. And He who sat on him was called Faithful and True, and in righteousness He judges and makes war.*

When Jesus is seen on His white horse, He comes to *judge* and then *make war*. To *judge* is judicial activity. *Making war* is battle-field. In other words, Jesus doesn't go to the battlefield until He has first set things in judicial order in the Courtroom. As a result of us not understanding this, we have potentially run to the bat-tlefield and not been effective. In fact, we may have even empow-ered the enemy in our presumption. If you challenge something without first removing its legal right through judicial activity, it can backfire against you. This could be the reason why in the midst of all our efforts since the mid-1990s we saw no real break-through but actually saw things go in the wrong direction. How-ever, God began to bring an awareness of the Courts of Heaven. We see the clearest picture of this Court in Daniel 7:9-10.

> *I watched till thrones were put in place,*
> *And the Ancient of Days was seated;*
> *His garment was white as snow,*
> *And the hair of His head was like pure wool.*
> *His throne was a fiery flame,*
> *Its wheels a burning fire;*
> *A fiery stream issued*
> *And came forth from before Him.*
> *A thousand thousands ministered to Him;*

> *Ten thousand times ten thousand stood before Him.*
> *The court was seated,*
> *And the books were opened.*

As Daniel *watched* in the spirit realm, he saw this Court. Daniel was looking into the *unseen* realm and *seeing* what was in operation there. Later in Daniel 7:25-27, Daniel sees this same *Court* in operation destroying and revoking the rights of the anti-Christ and its spirit.

> *He shall speak pompous words against the Most High,*
> *Shall persecute the saints of the Most High,*
> *And shall intend to change times and law.*
> *Then the saints shall be given into his hand*
> *For a time and times and half a time.*
> *But the court shall be seated,*
> *And they shall take away his dominion,*
> *To consume and destroy it forever.*
> *Then the kingdom and dominion,*
> *And the greatness of the kingdoms under the whole heaven,*
> *Shall be given to the people, the saints of the Most High.*
> *His kingdom is an everlasting kingdom,*
> *And all dominions shall serve and obey Him.*

Through the activity of this Court, the saints move from a place of defeat to a place of dominion and power. This didn't happen because of binding and loosing on the battlefield. It occurred because a decision was rendered from the Court of Heaven on behalf of the saints. I believe the same thing happened in November of 2016. The Court of Heaven out of a response from the case presented by the Church rendered a verdict that allowed Donald J. Trump to become the 45th President of the United States. This Court intervened in the destiny of a nation because a people had learned how to petition it and cry for mercy and God's purpose in a land.

We also see this same principle in the people of God never going to battle unless there was an offering presented on their behalf. For instance, Saul the first king of Israel would not go to battle without an offering speaking on behalf of him and the nation. Even though Saul understood the need for something to speak legally for him, he violated the protocol at that time by functioning as a priest when he was a king. Under the Old Covenant this was forbidden. Only under the New Covenant are we allowed to function as king and priest (see Rev. 1:5-6). Saul offered an offering to set things legally in place. The problem was this was only for Samuel to do. First Samuel 13:8-13 shows us a portion of this story.

> Then he waited seven days, according to the time set by Samuel. But Samuel did not come to Gilgal; and the people were scattered from him. So Saul said, "Bring a burnt offering and peace offerings here to me." And he offered the burnt offering. Now it happened, as soon as he had finished presenting the burnt offering, that Samuel came; and Saul went out to meet him, that he might greet him.
>
> And Samuel said, "What have you done?"
>
> Saul said, "When I saw that the people were scattered from me, and that you did not come within the days appointed, and that the Philistines gathered together at Michmash, then I said, 'The Philistines will now come down on me at Gilgal,

and I have not made supplication to the Lord.' Therefore I felt compelled, and offered a burnt offering."

And Samuel said to Saul, "You have done foolishly. You have not kept the commandment of the Lord your God, which He commanded you. For now the Lord would have established your kingdom over Israel forever."

The function of priests was to get legal things in place. This is why they would offer offerings to the Lord. These offerings would speak as testimony and grant God the legal right to bless. Then the kings could go to war and win because the judicial things were in place to allow it. The mistake Saul made was trying to function as both priest and king in his day. This was not allowed. He did, however, understand that you can't go to war if legal things are not first set in place. We as priests take the offering of the blood of Jesus and administer it into place on our behalf. We agree with the blood of Jesus and His activity as our High Priest. We silence every word and legal claim against us through agreeing with the testimony of Jesus' offering—His blood and body. This is done through repentance on behalf of ourselves, our forefathers, and our nation. When we do this, we are now ready to go to the battlefield and win. There is a whole process connected to this, but this is the principle that drives it. Our failure to understand the judicial necessity before the battlefield has cost us dearly in recent decades. We are seeking to see restoration come to our nation. We are in a critical time. Yet it would appear we now have a necessary piece of understanding we haven't had before.

This is what was done on behalf of Donald Trump before the November 2016 election. This is what I understood, and those who were with me. We were to accomplish this in the Courts of

Heaven to be a part of securing God's passion for America. We did this as I was instructed and requested in the dream.

It is helpful to be aware that scripture teaches that the spiritual unseen realm dictates and controls what goes on in the seen, natural world. Jesus said as much in John 5:19 when He was asked *how* the miracle healing of the man at the Pool of Bethesda occurred.

> *Then Jesus answered and said to them, "Most assuredly, I say to you, the Son can do nothing of Himself, but what He sees the Father do; for whatever He does, the Son also does in like manner.*

Jesus' answer to the query of how the miracle took place was that He simply did in the natural what He *saw* occurring in the spiritual realm. Jesus understood that the spiritual dimension controls the natural realm. We see the apostle Paul speaking from the same idea in Ephesians 6:12.

> *For we do not wrestle against flesh and blood, but against principalities, against powers, against the rulers of the darkness of this age, against spiritual hosts of wickedness in the heavenly places.*

Paul's statement reveals that he understood that any conflict he was in to see God's will done in the earth was spiritual in nature. In the unseen dimension there are high-ranking devilish powers seeking to resist God's will. If we are to see a physical manifestation of God's passion in the earth, we must *touch* something in the unseen. This is why Daniel *watched* in the unseen realm as the Court came to order. I knew this was what God was commissioning me to do on behalf of Donald Trump. We were, by faith, to step into this unseen place in the spirit world and *touch* something that would move things into order for Donald Trump to be elected. This is why he said to me in the dream, *"I need for you to shift things for me concerning the election."*

Remember that I was to gather with others on July 6 to shift things in the unseen spiritual realm so Donald Trump would be the Republican nominee and also win in the general election against Hilary Clinton in November of 2016. Even though it was Donald Trump in the dream *calling* me, I knew this was God's assignment for me and those who would gather. There was one concern I had—the date. July 4, of course, is a national holiday and celebration of our independence as a nation. My immediate thought was *why* do I have to do this conference on July 6 and risk a low turnout because of people being involved in Fourth of July festivities and celebrations? However, I knew the date was important; I just didn't know why until I did some research.

I discovered through some simple investigation, to my amazement, that July 6, 1854 was the day the Republican Party was birthed on the outskirts of Jackson, Michigan. Ten thousand people turned out for a mass meeting "Under the Oaks." From this initial gathering the Republican Party was born. One of the main platforms of this new party was the eradication of slavery. As I read this bit of information, I felt the Lord speak to me. He said, *"I intend to reclaim the Republican Party for My purposes."* This was why I needed to do this gathering on July 6th. God desired to restore what the Republican Party originally stood for. He didn't want to just get Donald Trump into the office of the presidency. The Lord also wanted to win back the Republican Party for now and the times to come. The Lord desires a party that can stand for His values and passions.

The truth is the Democratic Party has become increasingly anti-God and anti-Christ. It wants to paint itself as a party for the people. Yet it espouses policies and platforms that are diametrically opposed to the Lord and His standards. God intends for the Republican Party to be that which can fight against the Democratic Party's effort to remove God and the Lord Jesus from culture and society. I'm not saying the Republican Party has everything right. I am saying, however, that you have to be blind and deaf not to recognize that the Democrats have an agenda that is anything but godly. In the midst of the assignment I was given in this first dream, God wanted to set in motion the reclaiming of the Republican Party back to its roots and virtues as well as the election of Donald Trump.

In obedience to the dream we arranged the gathering to *shift things concerning election*. We scheduled a Thursday night through Saturday morning time to come before the Lord in His Courts. We had worship, prayer, preaching of the Word, and movement as we felt the Holy Spirit lead. Prior to the gathering I heard the Lord speak to me. He said, *"There will be a time in the gathering when I will invite you into My Counsel. When I do, I want you to decree James 1:11."* I didn't at this time really know what the *Counsel of the Lord* was. I was about to find out, however, and the power associated with this place in the spirit world.

Lord, as we come and position ourselves in Your Courts and the Counsel of the Lord, I thank You that You have a deep passion to restore America and the nations back to You. Lord, would You allow every evil intent of the devil and his powers to be revoked and removed. Allow, Lord, those You have chosen to take the places of leadership in our nations until these reflect more Your values than those of the devil. Please, Lord, raise leaders with Your heart to lead us away from the One World Order and back to Your will for each individual nation. Thank You so much for this. In Jesus' Name, amen!

Chapter 3

STANDING IN THE COUNSEL OF THE LORD

JEREMIAH 23:16-18 refers to the *Counsel of the Lord*. Jeremiah the prophet is actually contending with the false prophets of his day. He references the *Counsel the Lord* as a place that real prophets stand in.

> *Thus says the Lord of hosts:*
> *"Do not listen to the words of the prophets who prophesy to you.*
> *They make you worthless;*
> *They speak a vision of their own heart,*
> *Not from the mouth of the Lord.*
> *They continually say to those who despise Me,*
> *'The Lord has said, "You shall have peace"';*
> *And to everyone who walks according to the dictates of his own heart, they say,*
> *'No evil shall come upon you.'"*
> *For who has stood in the counsel of the Lord,*
> *And has perceived and heard His word?*
> *Who has marked His word and heard it?*

Jeremiah is making a distinction between himself and the false prophets. His point is that as a bona fide prophet he has stood and does stand in the Counsel of the Lord. The Counsel of the Lord is a realm of the spirit. In this dimension several things can happen. Before I talk about what this place is like in the spirit realm, let me explain that as New Testament believers we now have access into places in the spirit world that only prophets and priests could enter in the Old Testament. This is because as New Testament believers, God makes all His people prophetic. Acts 2:16-18 gives a clear-cut awareness of this reality.

But this is what was spoken by the prophet Joel:
"And it shall come to pass in the last days, says God,
That I will pour out of My Spirit on all flesh;
Your sons and your daughters shall prophesy,
Your young men shall see visions,
Your old men shall dream dreams.
And on My menservants and on My maidservants
I will pour out My Spirit in those days;
And they shall prophesy."

The prophetic essence of the Holy Spirit has been poured out on *all flesh*. The prophet Joel continues and declares that sons and daughters, young and old, servants both male and female will prophesy under this divine unction. In other words, everyone will have access into this realm of the prophetic that only prophets in the Old Testament could enter. So when I say that God would *invite* me into this Counsel, that doesn't mean I'm a prophet. It does mean, however, that I am prophetic in nature and have operated in a realm of faith that allows me to access this dimension.

To better understand where I was being invited into, let's look at the Counsel of the Lord. First of all the Counsel of the Lord and the Court of Heaven are different dimensions of the spirit realm. They are very similar, yet different in nature. I believe that many times we first operate in the Courts of Heaven then can stand and function in the Counsel of the Lord from the results of our Courtroom activity. The main difference between the Court of Heaven and the Counsel of the Lord is the presence or absence of the adversary. The adversary is not in the Counsel of the Lord. He, however, can be in the Courts of Heaven bringing accusation against us. This is why at times we enter the Courts of Heaven to answer any case the devil might be bringing against us, but then can step and stand in the Counsel of the Lord. From the Counsel, because every legal argument Satan was bringing is now answered, there can be functions that allow God's will to be done in the earth. Again, the Courts of Heaven and the Counsel of the Lord are very closely related. This is why when I was doing a conference and gathering regarding the election of Donald Trump as president, we first went into the Courts but ended up in the Counsel. In other words, what was accomplished in the Courts legally could now be implemented from the Counsel. To better understand this, let's look at some things that happen in and from the Counsel of the Lord.

First of all, the word of the Lord is heard. Again Jeremiah 23:18 unveils this.

> *For who has stood in the counsel of the Lord,*
> *And has perceived and heard His word?*
> *Who has marked His word and heard it?*

In the Counsel of the Lord the ability to perceive and hear the word of the Lord is available. In other words, we are standing in an atmosphere not just where God speaks, but where we can hear. Many times, God is speaking; we just aren't hearing. When we step into the Counsel of the Lord in this place it seems our hearing abilities are maximized. I become aware of *His word* coming to me in a way that perhaps I do not when I'm not standing in this place. It's the atmosphere of His presence and Counsel that empowers my hearing. Isaiah the prophet in Isaiah 50:4-5 speaks of having been given the *ear of the learned* and as a result the *tongue of the learned*.

The Lord God has given Me
The tongue of the learned,
That I should know how to speak
A word in season to him who is weary.
He awakens Me morning by morning,
He awakens My ear
To hear as the learned.
The Lord God has opened My ear;
And I was not rebellious,
Nor did I turn away.

The prophet, actually prophesying of Jesus the Messiah, speaks of the Lord opening and awakening his ear to hear. This happens in the Counsel of the Lord. Our ears become open and our hearts awakened to perceive His word we might otherwise miss. This is a precious place in the spirit realm as a result.

The next thing we are told can happen in the Counsel is the word of the Lord is *marked*. Again Jeremiah 23:18 gives us this insight.

For who has stood in the counsel of the Lord,
And has perceived and heard His word?
Who has marked His word and heard it?

To *mark* His word means to *prick up the ears*. In the Hebrew it is the word *qashab*. Mary and I have two small dogs. Their names are Otis and Abby. As with most people who have dogs, they are a significant part of the family. It is fun to watch them become attentive and aware when they hear the slightest sound that grasps their attention. Whether it's a siren, us speaking to them, or other sounds, you can visibly watch them turn their awareness to those sounds. They may turn their head as they try to figure out exactly what the sounds mean. At other times, according to the sound, they may wag their tail in pleasure that we are speaking to them. For instance, Otis in particular will be lying on the floor. We can say to him, "You're a good boy, aren't you?" His tail will wag as those words bring him pleasure. You can see his ears move as he *pricks* them up to listen to what his master says.

The same is true as we stand in the Counsel of the Lord. When we are there and hear the Lord, our ears in the spirit world prick up. We are listening intently to what the Lord as our Master is saying. When we are in the Counsel, quite often His words are assignments from this dimension we are to fulfill. The *pricking* up of our ears is a sign that we are listening diligently to the Lord and what He would speak to us in this place. Another thing I would draw our attention to concerning the Counsel of the Lord is it is a place we *stand* in. The word *stand* is the Hebrew word *amad*. It means to stand in a variety of ways. One of the definitions, however, means to *present yourself*. This is good. This is really what we do in the Counsel of the Lord. We present ourselves before Him. This is what Abraham did when he heard the voice of the Lord as God commanded him to offer Isaac as a sacrifice. Genesis 22:1 shows God speaking and calling Abraham's name. His response should be ours as well when we hear His voice.

> *Now it came to pass after these things that God tested Abraham, and said to him, "Abraham!" And he said, "Here I am."*

Abraham's response is simple yet honoring and full of intent to obey. When God calls him, Abraham answers with, *"Here I am."* In other words, "It doesn't matter what You are about to command me, I will do it no matter what." He doesn't qualify his response. He doesn't ask first, "What do You want?" He declares, *"Here I am."* In essence Abraham is saying, *"I am at Your disposal and will do whatever You request."* This is what it means to *stand*. This must be our posture in the Counsel of the Lord. We are presenting ourselves with absolute obedience in our hearts to fulfill the Lord's desire. From this posture of standing, there are other things that can occur in the Counsel of the Lord.

Another occasion in Abraham's life and walk with God shows us what can occur in the Counsel of the Lord. When God tells Abraham that He is about to destroy Sodom and Gomorrah, Abraham stands in the Counsel of the Lord to request a different decision. Genesis 18:22 shows Abraham standing before the Lord as God informs him He is going to destroy Sodom and Gomorrah.

> *Then the men turned away from there and went toward Sodom, but Abraham still stood before the Lord.*

Abraham positioned himself in between God and Sodom and Gomorrah. He stood there to intercede for this city and region. He sought to influence the heart of God and give Him the right He needed to be merciful. Abraham is standing in the Counsel of the Lord. Abraham and God *together* made the decision concerning this territory. God agreed with Abraham that if there were ten righteous He would spare it. This was the deal Abraham brokered with God for Sodom and Gomorrah. Genesis 18:32-33 shows this deal being set in place.

Then he said, "Let not the Lord be angry, and I will speak but once more: Suppose ten should be found there?" And He said, "I will not destroy it for the sake of ten." So the Lord went His way as soon as He had finished speaking with Abraham; and Abraham returned to his place.

The sad fact is there were not ten righteous. Therefore, Sodom and Gomorrah were destroyed. This does not negate, however, that Abraham did what he should have done. He stood in the Counsel of the Lord and interceded for this region. We too are called of God to stand before the Lord in His Counsel and seek to secure the destiny of cities, states, providences, regions, territories, nations and continents. The destiny of these and those who lead them are very much in the sphere of us as the church. We must take this very seriously and take our place before the Lord as Abraham did to see mercy come to nations and peoples. This is the power of standing in the Counsel of the Lord.

One more thing that can occur in the Counsel of the Lord is decrees can be made that shape the activity of nations. First Kings 17:1 shows us Elijah standing before Ahab, a wicked king of Israel. As he stands in this place as a prophet of God, he makes a decree from the spirit realm into the natural.

And Elijah the Tishbite, of the inhabitants of Gilead, said to Ahab, "As the Lord God of Israel lives, before whom I stand, there shall not be dew nor rain these years, except at my word."

Notice the wording that Elijah chose. He said, "*As the Lord God of Israel lives, before whom I stand.*" In other words, Elijah is saying to Ahab, "*Even as I stand before you in the natural, I am simultaneously standing before the Lord and His Counsel. From this Counsel I make a decree into the natural that it will not rain until I say so.*" Notice that this decree Elijah is making is from the Counsel of the Lord in which he is standing in the spirit world. This is where decrees have power. So often we seek to make decrees outside the Counsel of the Lord. I would boldly say that only decrees from within the Counsel of the Lord have power to perform. When Elijah made the decree of *no rain until I give it permission*, it happened for three and a half years because he set it in place from the Counsel of the Lord. This is the place in the spirit where we have the power to shape nations after the kingdom culture of the Lord. Elijah's decree from the Counsel of the Lord where he stood set judgements in place that did alter the future of a nation.

We have been commissioned by God to do the same. God would invite us into His Counsel to set in order His passion over America. This can determine the future of America. We as the people of God either take our place in the Counsel and the Courts of Heaven and establish this, or Satan and his hordes will determine what the future holds for America. I think your heart is like mine on this matter. I say, "*NEVER NEVER NEVER.*" We will take our place and determine what God's desire and will is over our land. This is what happened in the last election of President Donald J. Trump. I am set to see him become president again from the Courts and Counsel of the Lord. Let me tell you my story. Perhaps it might inspire and instruct us for this time we are in.

Lord, as we stand in Your Courts, we ask that all things would legally be set in place for Your will in America and the nations to be done. As this is accomplished, would You allow us as Your prophetic people to stand in Your

Counsel to decree a thing and see it fulfilled. Lord, we long to not default and abdicate our place before You. Lord, allow not the devil to determine the destiny of America and the nations. Lord, let Your church take its place before You and secure the future of America and the nations! In Jesus' Name, amen!

Chapter 4

ALL FLESH IS AS GRASS

A S we entered the gathering that had originated with Donald Trump calling me on the phone in my dream, remember the Lord had spoken to me. He had said, *"During the conference there will be a moment when I invite you into My Counsel. When I do, I want you to proclaim James 1:11."* I knew I had heard the Lord; however, I didn't understand some of the things I shared with you in the last chapter about the Counsel of the Lord. I didn't even really know at that time that the Courts of Heaven and the Counsel of the Lord were separate spiritual dimensions. I was just moving by faith in what I had heard. This is true for many of us. We have done many things under the leadership of the Holy Spirit not fully understanding them. Remember that one of the main functions of the Holy Spirit is to teach us to pray as we ought. Romans 8:26 tells us that He will help us in our weakness.

> *Likewise the Spirit also helps in our weaknesses. For we do not know what we should pray for as we ought, but the Spirit Himself makes intercession for us with groanings which cannot be uttered.*

When we don't know what or how we should pray, the Holy Spirit helps us in this weakness. He comes with understanding, revelation, insight, and unction to pray from. We become empowered to pray prayers that actually garner responses from Heaven. We must understand what the nature of real prayer is. Prayer is not trying to convince God to do something for us. Prayer is stepping into a spiritual dimension and agreeing and co-laboring with God to see things arranged in the spirit world for His will to be done on earth as it is in Heaven. We are not coming to beg or even make puny requests before God. We are coming to an elevated place granted to us by God to function there. As we do, we become a part of the process of God's will and passion being done in the earth. Isaiah 56:7 declares that we will be allowed to represent nations before the Lord in our prayers.

Even them I will bring to My holy mountain,
And make them joyful in My house of prayer.
Their burnt offerings and their sacrifices
Will be accepted on My altar;
For My house shall be called a house of prayer for all nations.

We as God's House of Prayer are to stand on behalf of nations. One of the most intriguing things about this is the word *prayer* in the Hebrew. It is the Hebraic word *tphillah*. It means supplication. The root of this word, however, is the Hebrew word *palal*. This word means *to judge!* Wow! Prayer is not just making requests of God. Prayer is standing in a place of the spirit and rendering judgements against anything that would resist the will of God. It is a place of great authority and power. This is what I was about to do in this gathering I was asked to convene. I didn't know it, but there was going to be a judgement from the Counsel of the Lord that would be necessary to Donald Trump being elected the United States president.

As I said, the Lord prior to the gathering had said He would invite me into His Counsel during the conference. When He did I was to *decree* James 1:11. This verse is a statement and judgement against those who arrogantly resist God.

For no sooner has the sun risen with a burning heat than it
withers the grass; its flower falls, and its beautiful appearance
perishes. So the rich man also will fade away in his pursuits.

As the conference progressed, we were functioning in the Court of Heaven. Through our worship, our offerings, the prophetic preaching of the Word, repentance, and our prayers, we were presenting ourselves in the Courts of Heaven. We were seeking to silence any voice against us in the Courts that would deny us the right to fulfill the assignment I had been given from the Lord to *shift things concerning the election in favor of Donald Trump*. Revelation 12:10-11 tells us there is an accuser of the brothers that operates against us before the Lord.

> *Then I heard a loud voice saying in heaven, "Now salvation, and strength, and the kingdom of our God, and the power of His Christ have come, for the accuser of our brethren, who accused them before our God day and night, has been cast down. And they overcame him by the blood of the Lamb and by the word of their testimony, and they did not love their lives to the death."*

The word *accuser* is the Greek word *katagoros*. It means *one who is against you in the assembly*. It also means a *complainant at law*. In other word it is one bringing a legal complaint against you. So the accuser of the brothers is not someone in the natural that is angry with you and speaking evil things about you. The accuser is a spiritual force and voice bringing legal accusations before the Throne of God against us day and night. They are perpetual in nature.

Again, I didn't know exactly what I was doing. I was simply moving in agreement with what I sensed the Lord doing. As we allowed the Holy Spirit to direct us, we ended up silencing the voices of the accuser from the Courts of Heaven against us that would've sought to deny us the right to fulfill and complete the assignment. Once this was done, I could then stand in the Counsel of the Lord and make the James 1:11 decree concerning the election of Donald Trump as president.

I remember so clearly as I stepped onto the platform after one of the speakers I had invited finished his message. In that moment I didn't just step onto a natural platform. I stepped into the Counsel of the Lord. I was very aware that I was now standing in a spiritual place and atmosphere of God's Counsel and all the activity there. I also knew this was the *place* from which I was to decree James 1:11.

Let me explain a little further concerning *how* I function primarily in the spirit realm. Many people I know are seers. In other words, they *see* into the realm of the spirit. They see images, movies, figures, and other pictures in their mind's eye. Some even would have open visions and the like. This is not how I primarily function. I'm much more a *hearer* and a *feeler*. In other words, I tend to discern what is happening in the spirit world by what I sense, feel, and hear rather than what I see. I do *see* at times but I'm much more proficient with the hearing and feeling. Sometimes what I am hearing and feeling will give birth to something I see. In other words, there is such a strong sensation coming from my spirit that it gives expression to me actually seeing something in the spirit world. However, my foremost means of picking up spiritual realities is through hearing and feeling.

Of course, hearing is when we have a thought or a *word* that is impressed on our minds and hearts. It's not that we actually hear a voice or a sound. We do, however, have an impression or idea that comes into our minds. This is the way the Holy Spirit speaks to us and we hear. I have found that the more I put the word of God into my mind and spirit, the more easily I hear. Jesus said that the Holy Spirit would cause me to *remember* what He had said. John 14:26 gives us an idea of how this operates.

> *But the Helper, the Holy Spirit, whom the Father will send in My name, He will teach you all things, and bring to your remembrance all things that I said to you.*

The Holy Spirit draws from the Word of God in our mind and spirit that we have placed there through the reading of His Word. At the opportune time that we need to *hear* a word from the Lord, He brings it to our remembrance. We are *hearing* from the Lord in these moments. This has happened many times to me. There are times when I am seeking to hear from the Lord and gain direction and a word from the scripture will be *quickened* or made alive to me. In Psalm 119:50 in the King James Version of the Bible, the word *quicken* is used.

> *This is my comfort in my affliction: for thy word hath quickened me.*

When we hear the Word of the Lord, it sparks something in our spirit. It's not the normal remembering process. When the Spirit of God speaks the Word of the Lord in our minds and spirits and causes us to remember, it brings faith. Romans 10:17 verifies this.

> *So then faith comes by hearing, and hearing by the word of God.*

We are told that when we *hear* the Word of the Lord, faith erupts in our hearts. As the Holy Spirit takes the Word of God and whispers it into our spirit, that spark that we feel is faith being energized in our hearts. We must learn to pay attention to this. This is one of the chief ways we *hear* from the Lord. As I stepped onto the platform that night, I knew I was standing in the Counsel of the Lord where I could *hear* the word of the Lord. What I heard from the Lord, I was to declare.

The other way I primarily pick up what is happening in the spirit realm is through feeling. The priest in the Old Testament determined the will of God through *feel*. In the breastplate of the priestly attire there was a pocket where the Urim and Thummim were. It is not exactly known what these were. It seems they were some kind of *stones* that the priest could *feel* and know what God was saying. Leviticus 8:8 tells us that these items were a part of the equipping of the priest.

> *Then he put the breastplate on him, and he put the Urim and the Thummim in the breastplate.*

First Samuel 28:6 tells us that King Saul, whom God had rejected as king, couldn't get any revelation from God. God would not answer him in any way, including through the Urim.

> *And when Saul inquired of the Lord, the Lord did not answer him, either by dreams or by Urim or by the prophets.*

In other words, when the priest put his hands into the breastplate to determine by *feel* the direction of the Lord, the Lord didn't answer. The idea is that we can know by feeling and sensing what the Lord is saying. This is a very strong way of perceiving the direction of the Lord. This is what is being implied when we are told the peace of God will guard our hearts and minds in Philippians 4:7.

> *And the peace of God, which surpasses all understanding,*
> *will guard your hearts and minds through Christ Jesus.*

We can tell by the presence of peace or the absence of it what God's will is. We are told that this peace *surpasses* understanding. In other words, we should be led more by what we *sense* than what we *see*. This is what was prophetically spoken of Jesus. Isaiah 11:3-4 tells us that Jesus' judgement and decisions were not based out of the natural realm of what He saw.

> *His delight is in the fear of the Lord,*
> *And He shall not judge by the sight of His eyes,*
> *Nor decide by the hearing of His ears;*
> *But with righteousness He shall judge the poor,*
> *And decide with equity for the meek of the earth;*
> *He shall strike the earth with the rod of His mouth,*
> *And with the breath of His lips He shall slay the wicked.*

Jesus' decision-making process was led by the spirit realm rather than the natural realm. He made decisions based on what He *sensed*, not by what He *saw*. This is living by what we are *feeling*. If we can pay attention to what we *feel* in the spirit we can discern what is happening in the unseen realm. We can begin to move accordingly and in sync with it. The result will be breakthrough.

This requires us to *trust* what we are feeling. Sometimes the natural things look so convincing and sure. Yet I have found when we believe more what we are sensing than seeing, it always plays out to be true.

This means that even when something seems to be *right* in the natural, but we *feel* something in the unseen realm, we must pay attention to this. The opposite is true as well. When something seems *wrong* in the natural but we have a peace about it and it feels right in the spirit, we should move forward. This is living by what we sense more than what we see. This is a primary way that God gives us direction. The word *guard* in Philippians 4:7 is the Greek word *phroureo*. It means a watcher in advance. In other words, the absence of peace or the presence of peace is declaring to us what is coming toward us. We can and should pay attention to this. We can be directed through the Holy Spirit by what we feel and we give place to this operation of the Spirit of God.

This is what I did as I stepped on to the platform that night and into the Counsel of the Lord. I had *heard* God say to declare James 1:11. I was now standing in the Counsel *sensing* an atmosphere of spiritual power and might I was to declare from. I had an awareness that what I declared in this moment would have lasting repercussions upon the coming election.

As I stood in this spiritual environment, I decreed: "*Lord, I declare that Hillary Clinton's campaign is as the grass of the field. I also declare that Hillary Clinton political* **campaign and agenda** *is as the flower of that field. Even as the burning, scorching, and exposing heat causes the grass to wither and fade, so I declare Hillary Clinton's campaign to wither away. I also declare that Your sun and heat will expose and cause to wither away Hillary Clinton's candidacy. She as the flower of the field will fade away and wither under Your burning* *and exposing heat. I declare that as a result, Donald Trump will be elected president of the United States."*

We all know what happened. Scandal and ridicule continuously overtook Clinton and her campaign. Even two weeks before the election, the FBI did another investigation of her and her activities. The result was she lost the election to Donald Trump. I understand that many others were praying. I do not discount this. However, I was given the assignment to decree from the Counsel of the Lord a judgement against Donald J. Trump's opponent. Just as Elijah decreed in his day that there would be no rain, we declared that all favor over Hillary Clinton's candidacy for president would dry up as exposure came concerning her and her campaign. We are not dealing with flesh and blood. This is not a prayer aimed at the person of Hilary Clinton. But there are people, like Clinton, who empower the advancement of demonic ideologies and principalities through their policies.

Another thing that happened just a little while before the FBI's last investigation of Clinton was my daughter had a dream. In her dream she saw the FBI beheading people. She was appalled and terrified by what she was seeing. She then saw the FBI behead an individual and lift up their head. It was the head of Hillary Clinton. As a result of our decree from the Counsel of the Lord, Clinton's head or authority and right to be president was taken off.

Figuratively, anytime someone's head is taken off it is being declared that they no longer have influence and authority. It is also being decreed they will not rise again. This is what happened when David took down Goliath. When the stone landed in his forehead and caused him to fall, David had to finish the job. Taking off his head was critical. It was a statement that the headship of the Philistines was now removed. Not only were they defeated, but the authority they functioned in was now revoked. First Samuel 17:51 shows that once the head was removed and it was known the *champion* was dead, the rest of the army fled and scattered.

> *Therefore David ran and stood over the Philistine, took his sword and drew it out of its sheath and killed him, and cut off his head with it. And when the Philistines saw that their champion was dead, they fled.*

The problem with our efforts to defeat ideologies, philosophies, ideas, and issues is we never take their head off. As with Goliath when David landed the stone in his forehead, they are addled, maybe knocked unconscious, but they aren't dead and definitely haven't had their head taken off. We need to finish the job. Otherwise they will rise again. In the political realm, the ones who espouse these concepts must be defeated and not allowed to be in office. Otherwise our victories will only be temporary. The head is still intact and will rally the troops again. We cannot stop prematurely. We must take the head of the thing off! David ran and seemed to stand on the huge body of Goliath, drew the giant's sword from his sheath, and took his head off. The armies of the Philistines fled because the head that drove the whole thing was now removed. The victory was sure.

When my daughter told me the dream, I knew we had *won*. The opponent of Donald J. Trump had been dismissed and we had an opportunity to recover America back to the destiny of God. A tragedy was averted and God showed mercy to America in giving us a season to repent and come back to the Lord. We, however, still need to make sure *the head* is off. It is yet there to be honest with you. This is why the re-election of Donald J. Trump is so imperative. We cannot stop prematurely. There is a *swamp* that still needs to be drained. The philosophy of socialism that promotes the One World Order through the empowerment of the anti-Christ spirit must have its head removed. In the next chapters, we will discuss the process for this and how we as the church must respond.

> Lord, we come by faith to stand in Your Courts and the Counsel of the Lord. Thank You that You empower our activities in this place to see spiritual unseen forces line up with Your will. We need Your grace to stand in these places and function appropriately and effectively. Thank You, Lord, for this grace to accomplish Your intent in the nation of America and the nations of the earth. Only by Your grace can this be done. In Jesus' Name, amen!

Chapter 5

DREAM NUMBER 2: SEATED IN THE CABINET

AFTER the election of President Donald J. Trump in November 2016 a great victory was won. I felt comforted that we had fulfilled our assignment to *shift things concerning the election* on his behalf. Little did I know that was only the first part of the assignment the Lord had for me.

Let me say here that I have a history of assignments to pray for the president of the United States. Even before I understood anything about the Courts of Heaven or the Counsel of the Lord, I had dreams and commissioning to stand with them in their functions. For instance, when George W. Bush was the president I had two dreams about him. The first was he came to *my house*. His purpose for coming to my house was I was supposed to *hide* him and protect him. I remember in the dream when he came to my house, I placed him in my *office* at the deepest corner away from everything for protection. I knew that I was being called to protect President Bush through my prayers and the authority I had in my office as an intercessor and apostle. As much as I understood it then, I endeavored to do this. The second dream I had about President Bush was he was flying in an airplane. As he flew, he crashed and became entangled in electrical or power lines. I knew that he was getting tangled in the political power lines in Washington D.C.

Most would believe that President Bush became incapacitated and did not fully accomplish what God desired through his presidency. He got tangled up in the power lines of politics. I am stating this to let it be known my history of assignments from the Lord in the function of our presidents. I know God has many whom He calls to this, but I am one of them. The call and assignment concerning President Trump is therefore not an unusual thing for me. However, I believe in this juncture of history so much more is hanging on the fulfillment of this assignment. If we drop the ball in this time, we may never see America recovered to her destiny. It is possible for something to be broken beyond remedy. Proverbs 29:1 warns of being destroyed without hope of healing.

> *He who is often rebuked, and hardens his neck, will suddenly*
> *be destroyed, and that without remedy.*

The United States of America is definitely one that has been rebuked, corrected, and chastened. Proverbs says that if in the process of this we don't repent and respond correctly by humbling ourselves, we can be destroyed and never recover again. The purpose God would have for a nation could be lost. This is why standing with President Donald J. Trump is so imperative. We cannot lose our nation to the forces desiring to overtake it. Our lives, but more importantly the lives, destinies, and futures of our children, grandchildren, and God's intent hang in the balance. We are contending for that which we cannot afford to lose. We must refuse to be broken with no remedy or answer for our destruction.

After the election of President Donald J. Trump but prior to his inauguration, I had a second dream. As in the first dream, now President-elect Donald J. Trump contacted me. This time, however, he didn't call me in my dream, but he came to me in person. He requested that I become a part of his cabinet that he was forming for his administration. The cabinet of a president consists of people who occupy *secretary* positions over certain high-ranking places of the government. For instance, the vice president is a part of this *cabinet* as well as the *secretary of state* who sees after foreign policy affairs and relates to foreign governments. There are many other *secretaries* as well. For instance, the secretary of energy, the secretary of housing, the secretary of education, and so forth. These all make up the cabinet that help a president govern the nation. There are additional people involved, but these are very high positions of influence and counsel to the president.

In my dream, President-elect Donald J. Trump came and asked me to be a part of his cabinet. I don't remember being asked to a specific position. I just knew he was requesting I take a place in the cabinet he would oversee and work with. I remember in the dream him saying to me, *"I know you probably don't have time, but I would like for you to do this."* It was as if he were politely asking but not requiring. There were two things I knew from this dream. One, I knew I was being asked by God, not President Trump, to stand in the Counsel of the Lord on behalf of President Trump and his cabinet and administration. I knew that having a *seat* in this cabinet was God giving me a place in the spirit world to intercede from the Counsel and the Courts of Heaven for President Trump and his administration. I also knew that because he mentioned me *not having time* to do it because of the busyness of my schedule, God was telling me to *make time!*

This was not something I actually had a choice in. In the midst of my travel, writing, ministering, and leading, this was to be a priority. God needed me to take this place/seat in *God's cabinet or Counsel* for President Trump and his cabinet/administration. Of course, as I considered this dream, I made a commitment to stand in the Counsel of the Lord and the Court of Heaven for President Trump and his administration. Every time I begin to pray concerning this, I immediately am in the Counsel of the Lord and/or the Courts of Heaven. It is as if the assignment grants me entrance there for the purpose of standing with and for President Trump. This is a result of having a *seat* in his cabinet. I may not have one in the natural, but I have a place in the spiritual dimension.

To understand the whole issue of a *seat* in the spirit realm, let me explain. Jesus promised in Revelation 3:21 that if we overcome we can sit in His Throne with Him.

To him who overcomes I will grant to sit with Me on My throne, as I also overcame and sat down with My Father on His throne.

Thrones are seats of government. In other words, we are promised a place of governmental authority that we can function in when we overcome. Prayers and other spiritual activities from these *seats* have great effect. Proverbs 20:8 shows us the power of sitting in a throne in the spirit world.

A king who sits on the throne of judgment scatters all evil with his eyes.

Just a look from one sitting as a king in a seat or throne will cause evil to scatter. The scripture says we are kings and priests to our God (see Rev. 1:6). So when we overcome and qualify to sit in a seat in the spirit realm, our activity there can have tremendous effect for the kingdom of God and its purposes. So in my dream, when I was asked to be in the cabinet of Donald J. Trump, I was being granted a seat in the spirit realm to function from. This is why, when I begin to pray for President Trump and his administration, I immediately am in another realm. I am in the Counsel of the Lord and/or the Court of Heaven. I actually take my seat and begin to function on behalf of the assignment God has given me and I have agreed to. It grants me a seat to work from. I can therefore pray prayers on an entirely different level. I can contend against that which is contending against President Trump. I can work with him in the spirit realm to see things come to divine order for God's purposes to be done through him. I am doing this from my seat granted to me by God.

As a result of this dream, I began immediately to stand before the Lord and take my seat in President Trump's *cabinet*. As I did this the Lord begin to speak to me. He told me that as I take my seat and function in this *cabinet* I must refer to President Trump as *my President Donald J. Trump*. As I felt and heard this (remember I am a hearer and a feeler primarily), I was at first confused. As I pondered it, however, it became clear what I was being asked to do. There was a reason *why* I had to operate this way before the Lord and the realm I was standing in. First of all, the Lord said I had to refer to Donald Trump as *my president*. The Lord told me when I did this, I was giving the Lord the right to move on President Trump's behalf. We must understand that what God will not do for some, He will do for others. God is no respecter of persons but He does move according to His own protocol. The truth of the matter is, God recognizes those He has called, chosen, and approved of. This is why Ezekiel 14:14-16 speaks of the righteousness of Noah, Job, and Daniel. Their righteousness wasn't enough to deliver their nation or their children but only themselves.

> *"Even if these three men, Noah, Daniel, and Job, were in it, they would deliver only themselves by their righteousness," says the Lord God. "If I cause wild beasts to pass through the land, and they empty it, and make it so desolate that no man may pass through because of the beasts, even though these*

three men were in it, as I live," says the Lord God, "they would deliver neither sons nor daughters; only they would be delivered, and the land would be desolate."

My point here is not what their righteousness couldn't do; it is that God was paying attention to them because of their righteousness. In other words, they had a power to pray prayers that only God would answer. The Lord said to me, *"The reason you must refer to Donald J. Trump as 'my' president is because that will give Me a right to do it for him. What I wouldn't or couldn't do for him, I will do for you."* This is not saying I am some special person. It is saying, however, that as I am faithful to the call of God and my assignment; I have a place to pray prayers that God will answer. As intercessors we must understand this principle. First John 5:16 tells us we can stand on behalf of those who have sinned and God will answer us for them.

If anyone sees his brother sinning a sin which does not lead to death, he will ask, and He will give him life for those who commit sin not leading to death. There is sin leading to death. I do not say that he should pray about that.

This is an amazing scripture. If we see someone sinning and we ask God, the Lord will show them mercy, not because they asked but because we asked on their behalf. This is not saying we can see someone saved by us asking for them. They must repent and ask God themselves. However, as they would move toward salvation, God will respond to them because we have a place in God and we asked. John does say, however, that if they have sinned a certain sin that no amount of our asking can solve that.

That would be the exception to the rule here. The main point, however, is that we have the right before God to make requests on behalf of another, because we are recognized in Heaven when they may not yet be. This is the place God gave me on behalf of President Trump. I'm not saying he isn't born again. I actually believe from the reports I have that he is. However, on the level of maturity he has as a believer he is not yet able to function in the spirit realm commiserate to his natural position. God needs others to stand on his behalf and do this. This is the place that I have been assigned to and granted.

The other thing I was told was to call him before God *Donald J. Trump*. I understood when this was said that this was significant and strategic before the Courts and Counsel of the Lord. There are many people in church in America who are believing God to turn President Trump into *John*. This is what the *J.* stands for in his name. *John* means the *beloved*. They feel that God would want to so regenerate President Trump that his nature as *the beloved of God* would manifest. I personally believe this is *not* the intent of God. We don't need a *beloved* as the President of the United States. We need a *Donald. Donald* means a *world-ruler!* The call on President Trump is not to be some soft, kind, and flexible person. The call on President Donald J. Trump is to change the world.

Let me explain. As I have mentioned, President Trump is challenging and dismantling the One World Order that has been propagated for decades. This is the attempt of the anti-Christ spirit to take over the world. This can never happen, however, with America as a super power. As long as America is strong the One World Order cannot proceed. This is why if it seemed that other administrations in America's history have worked to weaken America, it is not your imagination. This has been a thought-out and calculated plan to weaken America so there would be a willingness to have One World. Whether it is the weakening of our economy, open borders, godless rhetoric, or other emphasis, it is designed to bring America down so it can be controlled and manipulated for the purpose of the anti-Christ spirit. President Trump is a great hindrance to this endeavor. Therefore, he is hated and despised by those with this agenda. His *Make America Great Again* works against all *they* have been seeking to do for decades and generations. President Trump is God's servant against this devilish enterprise.

Another thing God is using President Donald J. Trump to do as a *world-ruler* is undo *political correctness. Political correctness* has been used to control the nations and promote the leftist agenda of One World dominance. Through *political correctness, they* have sought to silence people with opposing views. They have made it seem that those who held conservative views, biblical ideas, and traditional values were intolerant and bigots. This has been done through the propagation of *political correctness.*

What people don't realize is that *political correctness* is a thought-out strategy of *Marxism. Marxism* is the basis for communism, which flows out of socialism. *Socialism is a political and economic theory of social organization that advocates that the means of production, distribution, and exchange should be owned or regulated by the community as a whole.* In other words, the government of a nation owns and regulates all things. Individuals have nothing. They are themselves even *owned* by the State. The basis of all this is *Marxism*, originated by Karl Marx. The progress and promotion of *Marxism* has *political correctness* in its beginning strategies to overtake a culture.

President Donald J. Trump has been used by God to undo the *politically correct idea* that has dominated nations for decades. I hear many Christians and believers bemoan how crude and uncouth President Trump seems to be. They have a strong problem with him and the way he communicates, fights back, and expresses himself. They don't realize that part of their problem is they have been fashioned by the anti-Christ spirit that is pressing Marxism, socialism, and ultimately communism. They are a product of the politically correct spirit dominating culture and seeking to silence conservative and Judeo-Christian views. The imbedded political correctness in our society needs someone who will challenge it at its core. This someone is President Donald J. Trump. They can call him *unpresidential* in his speech, behavior, responses, and rhetoric all they want. The bottom line is God is using him to untangle political correctness from our culture. The end result will be a restoration of an ability to express our views without threat of retribution or ridicule. The voice of the true church will be free to arise and again speak and be an influence of culture in a nation.

When I pray and stand in the Courts of Heaven and the Counsel of the Lord as a part of President Donald J. Trump's *cabinet,* I ask that God would move on behalf of him, his cabinet, administration, and family. I ask and declare that *my President Donald J. Trump* would be blessed of God. The result of this is and will be the prosperity of my President Donald J. Trump and all his efforts aligned with God's purposes for America. I always ask that God would arise and defend His purposes in my President Donald J. Trump. I believe the result will be that God's plan for America will be reinstated and His passion fulfilled through our nation.

Lord, as we stand before Your Courts and Counsel, we ask that President Donald J. Trump would be blessed of You. We ask that Melania, Barron, Eric Trump and his family, Donald Trump Jr. and his family, Jared and Ivanka

Kushner and their family, and Tiffany would be blessed and kept by You. We ask that You might arise and defend Your purposes in President Donald J. Trump, his cabinet, administration, and family. We ask that every curse against him would be turned into a blessing. We ask that he and all connected to him would become stronger and stronger, while those who resist Your will through him will become weaker and weaker. In Jesus' Name, amen.

Chapter 6

Four Levels of Judgement

AS I have stood in the Counsel of the Lord and the Courts of Heaven for President Donald J. Trump, his family, cabinet, and administration, I have become aware of the judgement of God on his behalf. Psalm 2:1-6 shows us the principle of God setting His ruler and then contending for them from His Courts.

Why do the nations rage,
And the people plot a vain thing?
The kings of the earth set themselves,
And the rulers take counsel together,
Against the Lord and against His Anointed, saying,
"Let us break Their bonds in pieces
And cast away Their cords from us."

He who sits in the heavens shall laugh;
The Lord shall hold them in derision.
Then He shall speak to them in His wrath,
And distress them in His deep displeasure:
"Yet I have set My King
On My holy hill of Zion."

First of all, I am aware that this scripture is prophetic of Jesus and God setting Him as His King. However, there are also principles shown here that portray God's nature and heart toward any whom He seats as rulers of nations. Ultimately this is about Jesus and the attacks against Him. Yet they can also be about those God places who represent Him in the earth.

This is true of President Donald J. Trump. Because President Trump either wittingly or unwittingly is doing the will of God in our nation, the anti-Christ spirit detests him and wants to remove and unseat him. This is why there has been such talk of impeachment and other ideas of ridding President Trump from his office. Those who speak of such things have a problem, however. President Trump has been set by God. Notice that God *set* His King. When God *sets* someone they cannot not be removed. Others may fight and work against them, but they cannot be removed until God has finished His will in them and through them.

Notice also that the *nations rage and the people plot vain things*. This has happened in and with President Trump. There is great wrath at work against President Trump. I have never seen such anger and rage in all my life like what comes against him. This is nothing short of demonic and devilish. The rage with which people hate President Trump is not a human rage. It is the incited anger of the demonic against him and what God is accomplishing through him.

Notice also that there are *plots*. This word in the Hebrew is *hagah*. It means *to murmur and to ponder*. There are those who are constantly pondering ways to bring President Trump down. The liberal news media/fake news are always spinning stories, reports, interviews, and even outright lies to destroy this president.

We are witnessing before our very eyes Psalm 2 at work. They are in fact not just attacking President Trump but also the God he is representing, either knowingly or unknowingly. They are seeking to *break His bonds and cast away His cords*. The liberal, democratic, anti-God people desire to remove from the consciousness of a nation anything to do with God. They desire to make their own laws, rules, and philosophies to live by. God will not let this happen. This is why President Donald J. Trump is seated. God is set to defend him and His purposes in him.

This is why the rest of Psalm 2 speaks of the four levels of judgement that come on any people who set themselves against the Lord and in agreement with the anti-Christ spirit. The first level of judgement is *He who sits in the heavens shall laugh*. The second level of judgement, if there is no repentance, is *the Lord will hold them in derision* or *find them in contempt of Court*. The third level is *God will speak to them in His wrath*. The fourth level of judgement if there is no repentance is God will *distress them in His deep displeasure*. These four levels of judgement are against those who contend with God. Those who represent Him in the Courts of Heaven and the Counsel of the Lord should call for these judgements. In other words, we as those who would stand on behalf of God and His purposes in and through our leaders should agree with these judgements.

To fully get this idea we must know that the word *sits* in Psalm 2:4 is the Hebrew word *yashab*. It means to *sit down as a judge*. When the scripture says *He who sits in the heavens*, it is speaking of God in His seat as Judge of all the earth. So all four of the previous things mentioned are judgements that come from the Court of Heaven against those who would break His bonds and cast away His cords. These are renderings and sentences against those who rage and plot vain things to take down the one who has been set by God. We as the church, standing before the Lord as Judge, should ask for these judgements to be against those who conspire to do such things.

The first judgement is *God laughs*. About a month or so before voting day in America in November 2016, Mary, my wife, asked me what I thought would happen. She asked me if I thought Donald Trump would be elected president. Of course, all the polls said he would lose. All the *talking heads* on all the news programs said Hillary Clinton would be the first woman president of the United

States. They were celebrations planned. Even the anchors on the conservative TV network FOX News said they told their families they would be home early. Hillary Clinton would win and by a great margin. When Mary asked me what I thought, I told her what God had said to me. As I prayed the Lord said, *"He who sits in the heaven shall laugh."* In spite of all that was being reported, I knew that God was rendering a judgement on behalf of Donald Trump and against those who *imagined a vain thing.* When I told Mary what I thought, based on what I had heard she said, *"Do you think so?"* I said, *"Yes!"*

On the night of the election I took my place on my sofa to watch the election returns. As the returns began to come in, Donald Trump was winning. This was expected because of where some of the earlier returns were coming from. The reporters, however, cautioned everyone that this was where Donald Trump was always expected to win. They said the other states to report would begin to sway the election to Clinton. The problem was they didn't. Donald Trump won states he was *supposed* to win and then those states he wasn't *supposed* to win. The reporters, anchors, *experts,* and all the people in the media were flabbergasted, concerned, and even horrified. For most, their worst nightmare was being realized. How could such a thing happen?

As I sat and watched these returns and the response of the liberal media, I began to laugh. However, it wasn't just me laughing. I could feel God Himself laughing. He was mocking all those who had said they would break His bonds and cast away His cords. God was releasing the first of four judgements against those who would seek to deny the seat of president to the one He had chosen. As Judge, God was laughing at the preposterous idea that man could remove Him from their culture and society. When God laughs, those who are guilty of this will feel shame, humiliation, and ridicule. This is what I witnessed on all the liberal media outlets. There was a confounding, a humbling, and much anger. They were without an explanation. God had moved and set the one He had chosen to lead our nation. However, those who resisted were not about to repent. The fight was just beginning.

The next level of judgement is *God will hold them in derision or contempt of Court*. Remember that God is *sitting* as a Judge in this situation. The word *derision* is the Hebrew word *laag*. It means to *imitate a foreigner and to speak unintelligently*. God begins to ridicule and make fun. He mocks them. Some believe that because God is doing this as the Judge, He is finding them in contempt of Court. Contempt of court is what happens when someone in a court setting does not give due honor and respect to the Judge or the Court He oversees. This is when someone is found in *contempt of court*. This usually results in jail time and a fine. It is usually not a lengthy sentence but enough to get the person functioning in the court's attention. If people do not humble themselves under the ridicule and laughter of the One who sits as Judge, they can be found in contempt of Court and be derided. The whole purpose of this process is to bring them to repentance. In America this has yet to happen. Therefore, we as the church and those called to stand in President Donald J. Trump's *cabinet/counsel* must continue to call for the Judge's judgement.

The third level of judgement is *God speaks in His wrath*. This word *wrath* is the Hebrew word *aph*. It means to *breath out the nostrils with passion*. It means *rapid breathing with passion*. Clearly this is saying that if they do not repent after the first two judgements, God will become angry and begin to breathe out words of judgement. God's words toward those who would cast away His cords and remove and seek to break His bands are designed to cause them to reconsider their ways. His words are the last warning before the judgement of displeasure and distress is released. This is what happened to Nebuchadnezzar in Daniel 4:27-31. He was warned by a dream that Daniel interpreted. He was told judgement would come if he did not acknowledge the Lord God. This is what happened.

> "*Therefore, O king, let my advice be acceptable to you; break off your sins by being righteous, and your iniquities by showing mercy to the poor. Perhaps there may be a lengthening of your prosperity.*" *All this came upon King Nebuchadnezzar. At the end of the twelve months he was walking about the royal palace of Babylon. The king spoke, saying, "Is not this great Babylon, that I have built for a royal dwelling by my mighty power and for the honor of my majesty?" While the word was still in the king's mouth, a voice fell from heaven: "King Nebuchadnezzar, to you it is spoken: the kingdom has departed from you!*"

Daniel warned him to repent so that the days of his tranquility could continue. Notice that he appeared to him for 12 months. However, the arrogance of his heart was not dealt with. When he spoke and believed how great he was apart from God, judgement came. This was God speaking in His wrath before the distressing came. If people do not repent during this third warning coming from the wrath of God, the fourth realm of judgement will fall.

The fourth level of judgement is to be *distressed in His deep displeasure*. The Hebrew word *charown* is the word *displeasure*. It means to be full of fury. We have moved from God laughing, to Him deriding, to Him breathing with passion, to now a fury and a burning with anger. Once this level hits, full judgement is coming. Every time I think about the words *distress in His deep displeasure*, I think about the Egyptian army chasing the Jews into the parted Red Sea. The Bible says God *troubled* them. Exodus 14:24-28 shows how God destroyed those who persecuted His people and His purpose in them.

> *Now it came to pass, in the morning watch, that the Lord looked down upon the army of the Egyptians through the pillar of fire and cloud, and He troubled the army of the Egyptians. And He took off their chariot wheels, so that they drove them with difficulty; and the Egyptians said, "Let us flee from the face of Israel, for the Lord fights for them against the Egyptians."*
>
> *Then the Lord said to Moses, "Stretch out your hand over the sea, that the waters may come back upon the Egyptians, on their chariots, and on their horsemen." And Moses stretched out his hand over the sea; and when the morning appeared, the sea returned to its full depth, while the Egyptians were fleeing into it. So the Lord overthrew the Egyptians in the midst of the sea. Then the waters returned and covered the chariots, the horsemen, and all the army of Pharaoh that came into the sea after them. Not so much as one of them remained.*

The Lord fought for His people. He troubled or distressed the Egyptians in His deep displeasure. The chariot wheels fell off of what they were driving. The end result was the whole army drowned in the Red Sea. The Israelites never had to worry about the Egyptians again. They were forever defeated before them. So we should pray in our nation. We should pray that the judgement of God would come on all who would seek to cast away His cords, break His bands, and remove and seek to unseat Donald J. Trump. We must stand and pray that God's judgement would be rendered against all who would fight against God and His purposes in and through President Donald J. Trump. This is not calling fire down from Heaven on people or wishing harm upon anyone. This is, however, recognizing the anointing on President Trump, the unique assignment God has called him to, and taking our place as intercessory voices representing and protecting him in the heavenly realm where we take a firm stand against the demonic agenda to remove him from power.

As we pray this way, I believe we will witness the purposes of God being restored to America. We can see His will and passion come to pass in our nation.

Here is a prayer to pray for God's judgement that produces divine order for our nation.

Lord, as we stand as Your church before Your Courts, we acknowledge that You are the One who sits in the heavens. You, Lord, are the Judge of all the earth. Lord, we believe that already judgements have begun to come from Your Throne. These judgements are not designed to destroy but to reclaim nations to their God-ordained destinies.

Lord, we thank You that You have set President Donald J. Trump. He is firmly established as the one You have chosen. We ask, Lord, as Your church that all efforts to unseat him come to nothing. We ask that what You have decreed will be the final word concerning President Donald J. Trump. We thank You that he will complete this first term and be re-elected for the second term. The heathen will rage, Lord, but Your will will be done.

Lord, You have laughed and continue to laugh in mockery at the enemy, the anti-Christ spirit. We thank You that this spirit is judged by You. That which has come to ridicule, You, Lord, have ridiculed.

Thank You, Lord, that You have found this spirit and those who agree with it in contempt of Court. For the sake of Your Court's authority and influence, You are setting sanctions in place against those who have held You and Your Court in contempt. Lord, let it be known that You are the God in Heaven and You rule in the affairs of men.

Lord, we also ask that You would now speak in Your wrath to these who would seek to cast Your influence away. Arise, O God, and defend Your purposes in the earth through Your chosen vessels. Let Your will be done on earth even as it is in Heaven. Speak and bring these to repentance if possible even as You did Nebuchadnezzar. Let them *"kiss the Son, lest He be angry and they perish from the way."*

Finally, Lord, should they not repent, distress them in Your deep displeasure. Let them not claim the nations for the purposes of the anti-Christ. Arise, O God, and defend Your will and passion in the nations. We humbly stand before You and request this for the sake of Your desire in the earth. Let not our nation perish from the way, but let it be established as "One nation under God, indivisible, with liberty and justice for all." Restore us, O God, we pray!

Chapter 7

DREAM NUMBER 3: RUNNING MATE

R IGHT after President Donald J. Trump's inauguration, I had my third dream. In this dream President Trump came to me and asked me to be his *running mate* for the 2020 election. When I awoke, the dream puzzled me. After all, President Trump was just *beginning* his first four-year term as president. Very quickly, however, God spoke to me. He said, *"What I intend to do through President Trump will take eight years to do. I need you to 'run with him in the spirit as his running mate' to move everything into divine order for him to be re-elected."*

I have endeavored to do this. My intercession for him in the Courts of Heaven and the Counsel of the Lord has been to keep him from being *unseated* by the anti-Christ spirit and to see him *reseated* for his second term. This is what I am in the midst of as I write this book. I am endeavoring to *run with President Donald J. Trump* for this to be accomplished. I am also seeking to enlist those of like heart to join me in the spirit realm and strategic meetings across America to see this done. I understand that any legal right the devil might claim to work against the declared will of God must be dismantled. We must contend from the Court of Heaven for the devilish intent of the anti-Christ spirit to be thwarted. We see what this demonic thing is after in Daniel 7:25-28.

"He shall speak pompous words against the Most High,
Shall persecute the saints of the Most High,
And shall intend to change times and law.
Then the saints shall be given into his hand
For a time and times and half a time.
But the court shall be seated,
And they shall take away his dominion,
To consume and destroy it forever.
Then the kingdom and dominion,

And the greatness of the kingdoms under the whole heaven,
Shall be given to the people, the saints of the Most High.
His kingdom is an everlasting kingdom,
And all dominions shall serve and obey Him."
This is the end of the account. As for me, Daniel, my
thoughts greatly troubled me, and my countenance changed;
but I kept the matter in my heart.

This is describing the anti-Christ spirit that would work against the purposes of God. This is what is driving the One World Order and therefore the leftist movement in nations. As present-day believers, we need an understanding of the anti-Christ spirit in operation. First John 4:1-5 grants insight into the function of this spirit.

Beloved, do not believe every spirit, but test the spirits,
whether they are of God; because many false prophets have
gone out into the world. By this you know the Spirit of God:
Every spirit that confesses that Jesus Christ has come in the
flesh is of God, and every spirit that does not confess that
Jesus Christ has come in the flesh is not of God. And this is
the spirit of the Antichrist, which you have heard was com-
ing, and is now already in the world.

You are of God, little children, and have overcome them,
because He who is in you is greater than he who is in the
world. They are of the world. Therefore they speak as of the
world, and the world hears them.

We are told that the anti-Christ spirit is mainly typified by denying that Jesus Christ has *come* in the flesh. At the basis concerning this spirit is the deception that Jesus is not the Son of God and the Messiah of the world. We know there are groups, religions, and people who question this. They definitely are under the control and influence of the anti-Christ spirit. However, this spirit's influence is much more sinister than this. It is not as cut and dried as if someone simply doesn't believe Jesus is the Messiah. It goes further than this. Notice that this spirit propagates that Jesus Christ hasn't *come* in the flesh. This word *come* is the Greek word *erchomai,* and its idea is not just what has *come, but what is coming.* The scripture says they don't just "not confess" that Jesus Christ has come in the flesh, but that He is yet not coming. The anti-Christ spirit denies that Jesus Christ the Anointed Messiah came. This spirit, however, denies that Jesus the Christ, the Messiah, is now manifesting who He is through us the church. In other words, this spirit doesn't just deny who Jesus is, it denies who we are *in* Jesus! First Corinthians 12:12 tells us that we are *the* body of *Christ* in the Earth.

> *For as the body is one and has many members, but all the members of that one body, being many, are one body, so also is Christ.*

Christ is a many-membered body. We are here revealing, manifesting, and demonstrating the nature, power, and life of Jesus presently. The anti-Christ spirit's ambition is to deny, discredit, and denounce not only who Jesus is but who we are as well as His representatives. This is why there is such a fight in our culture. This is why the persecution continues to intensify. It is the anti-Christ spirit seeking to remove any ideas, concepts, people, and movements that declare and proclaim who Jesus is as the Christ. This spirit will not rest until any ideas of God and Jesus His Son are squelched. It is our job, however, to stand with boldness against this spirit and declare the witness of the Lord in the earth.

Notice that according to First John 4:1-5 we have the power to overcome those who are governed by this spirit. This is because the Holy Spirit of God in us, bearing witness to Jesus, is greater than this anti-Christ spirit that is in the world. The spirit that is in the world cannot overcome the Spirit of God within us. Notice also that *false prophets* operate under this power of this spirit. Anyone who does not make Jesus the central theme of their voice and words should be looked upon with scrutiny. I am speaking of those who purport to be Christian ministers. If what they preach is not lifting up Jesus and what He has done and is doing on our behalf, they could be under the influence of this spirit. This is why the apostle Paul warned against *another gospel* being preached. Galatians 1:6-9 speaks of this the gospel that was being espoused.

> *I marvel that you are turning away so soon from Him who called you in the grace of Christ, to a different gospel, which is not another; but there are some who trouble you and want to pervert the gospel of Christ. But even if we, or an angel from heaven, preach any other gospel to you than what we have preached to you, let him be accursed. As we have said before, so now I say again, if anyone preaches any other gospel to you than what you have received, let him be accursed.*

Paul was being emphatic about guarding themselves against an offshoot of the gospel. A *gospel* that was a *version* of the real gospel of the Lord Jesus Christ was not to be received. This was an expression of the anti-Christ spirit that would draw people away from the centrality of who Jesus is and who we are in Jesus. In the midst of a culture directly attacking what is *Christian,* we also have those within the church who would lead people away from Jesus. We must fight and war for the purity of the gospel. This is what we are also warned of in Second Corinthians 11:3-4.

> *But I fear, lest somehow, as the serpent deceived Eve by his craftiness, so your minds may be corrupted from the simplicity that is in Christ. For if he who comes preaches another Jesus whom we have not preached, or if you receive a different spirit which you have not received, or a different gospel which you have not accepted—you may well put up with it!*

Paul again is warning the church not to allow the *preaching of another Jesus or gospel.* Notice that Eve was *corrupted from the simplicity in Christ.* We cannot allow the purity and non-manipulated gospel to be lost. We must war for the *simplicity* that is in Christ. The purity of walking in union, fellowship, and communion with Him and a love for His Word, Spirit, and people. When Satan questioned this with Eve and she bought into it, all was lost. We must guard the simplicity of loving Jesus and His purity. This is what the early church walked in and what made them so powerful. Acts 2:46 speaks of this single-hearted and simple mindset.

> *So continuing daily with one accord in the temple, and breaking bread from house to house, they ate their food with gladness and simplicity of heart,*

We mustn't allow the anti-Christ spirit to sabotage our faith and lead us away from the simplicity of serving the Lord Jesus Christ. We are to be madly in love with Him and serving Him with all our heart. The anti-Christ spirit and those who would preach, teach, and prophesy from it must be fought against and not allowed a place in the church. To do so is to allow this spirit to take ground and erode away that which is necessary to the purposes of God in our lives and culture.

The other thing mentioned in First John 4:1-5 is that the world *hears* and pays attention to this spirit because the world is under its sway. The things spoken by this anti-Christ spirit make no sense to true believers and even those who are of conservative values. It is amazing how people can be drawn in to the ideas that are being put forth. All the genders that now are accepted, when we know God made two, male and female. Open borders that would let anyone in and vote even as illegal aliens. Paying for everyone's college and whatever else when it is virtually impossible to do so. There isn't enough money. This would mean an unbelievable tax hike that would cripple the American economy. This flows from an entitlement mindset that is socialistic in its roots. Things that are being promised and spoken of have no foundation in reality. Yet this spirit drives it and those who are under its ideology grasp it and call it innovative and ground-breaking. To allow this idea into place is to sow the deception that will bring ultimate destruction to America and the nations. This is what we are pushing against. We must continue our fight to see God's standards in place on a personal level and a national level. Psalm 11:3 gives us a dire warning.

If the foundations are destroyed, what can the righteous do?

It is the job of us the church to be the salt of the earth and the light of the world to not allow this to happen. In Matthew

5:13-14, Jesus instructs us to take our place of influence and not allow the foundations to be destroyed.

> *You are the salt of the earth; but if the salt loses its flavor,*
> *how shall it be seasoned? It is then good for nothing but to be*
> *thrown out and trampled underfoot by men. You are the light*
> *of the world. A city that is set on a hill cannot be hidden.*

We as the salt cannot lose our flavor. One of the reasons why nations are in the shape they are in is because the church lost its saltiness. We must regain it and stand up with the influence we are called to. We also must be the light of the world and let our light of influence for Jesus and His values shine forth. If we do not, the anti-Christ spirit will win. The foundations of society will crumble and we and our children to come will suffer. We must contend in this day for righteousness to reign. We must repent of our lack of duty that we have shown and seek to regain it. These are imperative days. We cannot be asleep. We must awake and shine forth like never before. Our time and the time of our children, grandchildren, and beyond demand it. This anti-Christ spirit must not be allowed to rule!

> Lord, as we stand before Your Courts and in Your Counsel, we ask that every agreement with the anti-Christ spirit would be annulled. We ask that in any and all places we have participated with this spirit our repentance would be accepted. Forgive us for our arrogance and turn us again to You. We cannot be a part of bringing down this spirit if we are agreeing with it. We by faith repent for all agreements and ask that any rights it is claiming against

us are now revoked and removed. Lord, we request judgement against this spirit that is working against America and the nations. Lord, let Your judgement now come and Your divine order be established again. Lord, we are in desperate need of You. In Jesus' Name, amen!

Chapter 8

BEHOLD THEIR THREATENINGS

WHEN we talk of the anti-Christ spirit, we are speaking of that which seeks to intimidate through threatenings. We see this today. They will market in fear and panic to try and control the culture. This is one of the biggest strategies of this spirit. We see this going on in regard to President Donald J. Trump. Everything from him being unbalanced and crazy to the idea he is going to start a nuclear war and everything in between. There is nothing but negative reporting about this president by the liberal media. It is designed to create a big question mark and create fear in the minds of people in America and the world. This is nothing new. This is what this spirit did in the days of the early apostles. When Peter and John were used to heal the lame man at the Gate Beautiful in Acts 3, they were then brought into questioning by the authorities of that day. They were commanded not to speak anymore in the Name of Jesus. When they were let go, they returned to their company of believers in Acts 4:23-31 and began to pray. This prayer has some insight into their awareness of the anti-Christ spirit they were contending with.

And being let go, they went to their own companions and reported all that the chief priests and elders had said to them. So when they heard that, they raised their voice to God with one accord and said: "Lord, You are God, who made heaven and earth and the sea, and all that is in them, who by the mouth of Your servant David have said:

"'Why did the nations rage,
And the people plot vain things?
The kings of the earth took their stand,
And the rulers were gathered together
Against the Lord and against His Christ.'

"For truly against Your holy Servant Jesus, whom You anointed, both Herod and Pontius Pilate, with the Gentiles and the people of Israel, were gathered together to do whatever Your hand and Your purpose determined before to be done. Now, Lord, look on their threats, and grant to Your servants that with all boldness they may speak Your word, by stretching out Your hand to heal, and that signs and wonders may be done through the name of Your holy Servant Jesus."

And when they had prayed, the place where they were assembled together was shaken; and they were all filled with the Holy Spirit, and they spoke the word of God with boldness.

As they prayed, they quoted Psalm 2. Remember that Psalm 2 is the word where the nations are raging and the people are plotting vain things against the Lord and His Christ. This is the anti-Christ spirit. As they pray, they begin to point out to the Lord the *threats* that have been leveled at them. This is always the ploy of this spirit. It will seek to control through intimidation and threats. It will seek to *put us back into our place* by intimidation and fear. We must be wise, but not allow this spirit to do this. Its purpose is to silence us and our voice of influence. We must fight back against this spirit and allow our voice to be heard. This will cause attacks but will also encourage others to stand and be heard. Philippians 1:12-14 shows the apostle Paul being aware that what he was going through was encouraging others to speak up.

But I want you to know, brethren, that the things which happened to me have actually turned out for the furtherance of the gospel, so that it has become evident to the whole palace guard, and to all the rest, that my chains are in Christ; and most of the brethren in the Lord, having become confident by my chains, are much more bold to speak the word without fear.

Paul was rejoicing that the hardship and persecution he had endured was being used by God to make others bold. This is what happens when we refuse to let the anti-Christ spirit silence us. Others will find their voice and begin to sound forth. They will realize they are not the only ones. We must not be silenced through intimidation. In fact, we can take the intimidation and present it as a case in the Courts of Heaven. David did this when Shimei came out cursing him as he fled from Absalom. Second Samuel 16:5-12 shows Shimei accusing, cursing, and threatening David. Notice David's response in the moment.

Now when King David came to Bahurim, there was a man from the family of the house of Saul, whose name was Shimei the son of Gera, coming from there. He came out, cursing continuously as he came. And he threw stones at David and at all the servants of King David. And all the people and all the mighty men were on his right hand and on his left. Also Shimei said thus when he cursed: "Come out! Come out! You bloodthirsty man, you rogue! The Lord has brought upon you all the blood of the house of Saul, in whose place you have reigned; and the Lord has delivered the kingdom into the hand of Absalom your son. So now you are caught in your own evil, because you are a bloodthirsty man!" Then Abishai the son of Zeruiah said to the king, "Why should this dead dog curse my lord the king? Please, let me go over and take off his head!"

But the king said, "What have I to do with you, you sons of Zeruiah? So let him curse, because the Lord has said to him, 'Curse David.' Who then shall say, 'Why have you done so?'"

And David said to Abishai and all his servants, "See how my son who came from my own body seeks my life. How much more now may this Benjamite? Let him alone, and let him curse; for so the Lord has ordered him. It may be that the Lord will look on my affliction, and that the Lord will repay me with good for his cursing this day."

When Zeruiah wanted to justify his king and take the head of Shimei off, David wouldn't let him. David said, *"Let him curse. Maybe God will look on what is happening to me now and repay me with good."* This is basically what Peter, John, and the people did in Acts 4. They said, *"Lord, behold their threats."* They were calling God's attention to the threats and asking for a judgement in their favor from the Courts of Heaven. The result was the place they were in was shaken and God began to stretch out His hand and do many signs and wonders to combat this anti-Christ spirit that wanted to dominate. We must know, if we can come before the Lord and get a judgement against this spirit from the Courts of Heaven, we can see God's purposes done. This is what happened in Daniel 7:25-28. The Court of Heaven rendered a verdict and the anti-Christ spirit's right to influence and operate was revoked. We need this today in America and the nations of the earth. Let's look at this anti-Christ spirit and its wicked operation in Daniel 7.

Notice the things this spirit will do, and see if this doesn't describe the present state of things. First of all, *he* will speak against the Most High. Daniel 7:25 shows this spirit setting itself against God Himself. This spirit and the people it controls attack God Himself.

> *He shall speak pompous words against the Most High,*
> *Shall persecute the saints of the Most High,*
> *And shall intend to change times and law.*
> *Then the saints shall be given into his hand*
> *For a time and times and half a time.*

This is exactly what Satan did when he was yet Lucifer in Heaven. It is his very evil and wicked nature. Isaiah 14:12-15 shows the intent of Satan while yet in Heaven as Lucifer sought to exalt himself above God. What audacity.

> *How you are fallen from heaven,*
> *O Lucifer, son of the morning!*
> *How you are cut down to the ground,*
> *You who weakened the nations!*
> *For you have said in your heart:*
> *"I will ascend into heaven,*
> *I will exalt my throne above the stars of God;*
> *I will also sit on the mount of the congregation*
> *On the farthest sides of the north;*
> *I will ascend above the heights of the clouds,*
> *I will be like the Most High."*
> *Yet you shall be brought down to Sheol,*
> *To the lowest depths of the Pit.*

The sin of Lucifer was to exalt himself above God and try to be like Him. This is why he speaks pompous words against the Most High. He is speaking evil and seeking to pull Him down, that he might be exalted. This is always the intent of the anti-Christ spirit. It will seek to exalt itself above God. It wants the place of God Himself. This is why it attacks God and anything resembling the Most High. This is why the normal, right values that the earth stands on are under attack. It is this spirit seeking to bring God down and all things from Him. As with Lucifer in Heaven, however, it will not work. Remember, God who sits in the heavens will laugh. We must stand with the Lord and against this spirit of anti-Christ to protect and defend the purposes of God in the earth. With a vengeance against Satan and this anti-Christ spirit, we must arise and fight for our King and His desires in our nation.

Another thing this spirit does is attack the saints of the Most High.

He shall speak pompous words against the Most High,
Shall persecute the saints of the Most High,
And shall intend to change times and law.
Then the saints shall be given into his hand
For a time and times and half a time.

Remember that the anti-Christ spirit doesn't just deny Jesus and who He is but those of us who belong to Jesus and who we are in Him. This spirit will seek to persecute and wear us out so we lose a passion to continue the fight. We mustn't allow this to happen. We must be driven forward by the impetus of the Spirit of God in us. If He can stop and thwart us, the purposes of God will be lost in the earth. If we will fight, the Lord will arise to defend us. We must continuously present our case in the Courts of Heaven, that a judgement might be rendered to revoke the rights of the spirit. When we do, our nations will be reclaimed to the Lord.

The next thing mentioned is this spirit *intends* to change times and laws. This can mean several things but it means among others that this anti-Christ spirit wants to restructure society. The principles and traditions that have governed for centuries, it wants to undo. The foundations society is built on, it desires to remove. One of the premises of the left's agenda is that we need to become a *current* people. In other words, we don't need to be stuck in *archaic days*. They say the principles and traditions that have governed us, we have now outlived. This is preposterous. It is a ploy to gain the support of a generation who are filled with entitlement ideas and don't have a history to see through these concepts. We must fight this. Laws that have governed us based on the Word of God must be kept intact. We haven't outlived the days of the standards of God. We refuse to allow this anti-Christ spirit to change times and laws and restructure the societies we live in. We come before the Courts of Heaven and declare Psalm 119:126.

It is time for You to act, O Lord, for they have regarded Your law as void.

Arise, O God, and judge that which would pervert Your law and that which has been set for centuries. Defend, O God, Your purposes in the earth. If we as His people will appeal to His Courts, a judgement will be rendered to defend His purposes in our nations, culture, and societies.

Notice that once the Courts render a judgement on behalf of the saints and God's purposes, dominion is set in place in the earth. Daniel 7:26-28 chronicles this.

"But the court shall be seated,
And they shall take away his dominion,
To consume and destroy it forever.
Then the kingdom and dominion,
And the greatness of the kingdoms under the whole heaven,
Shall be given to the people, the saints of the Most High.
His kingdom is an everlasting kingdom,
And all dominions shall serve and obey Him."

This is the end of the account. As for me, Daniel, my
thoughts greatly troubled me, and my countenance changed;
but I kept the matter in my heart.

The saints go from a place of *defeat* to a place of *dominion*. This happens because there is a people who knows how to appeal to the Courts of Heaven on behalf of their nation. This is what we are doing on behalf of America. We understand that the re-election of President Donald J. Trump is essential to this. We are contending for this as we *run with him in the spirit*. We are functioning as his *running mate* to see all things moved into place for God's passion to be fulfilled. Will you *run with us* for the sake of God's plan for America and your nation? I hope so!

Lord, as we stand before Your Courts, we ask for Your judgement against the anti-Christ spirit that would seek to change times and laws and restructure society. It is time, Lord, for You to arise and to judge those who would make void Your law. Arise, God, and defend Your purposes in the nation of America and the nations of the earth. For the earth is the Lord's and the fulness thereof, the world and all those who dwell therein. Thank You, Lord, for reclaiming all that has been given to You through covenant. We ask this from Your Courts and the Counsel of the Lord. In Jesus' Name, amen!

Chapter 9

Partnering with God

THERE is something I call a *hyper-view of the sovereignty of God*. This is where people think whatever God wants will happen because God desires it. This is not true. In fact, the idea that God is in *control* of the earth is wrong. God is not in *control*. He is in *charge*, but not in *control*. This may be a shocking statement. Let me explain. If God is in *control* this would mean that He is to blame for all the troubles, tragedies, and travesties that have happened and are happening. He is not. He is, however, in *charge* but has dedicated the stewardship of the earth to the sons of men. Psalm 115:16 declares the stewardship of the earth is under men's control.

> *The heaven, even the heavens, are the Lord's; but the earth*
> *He has given to the children of men.*

God claims the heavens for Himself, but the earth He gave to us as the human race. This is why Adam was put in charge of the planet alongside Eve. Any trouble on the earth is the result of man's control, not God's. However, God is still in charge in that He is upon His Throne ruling all things. What this means is that, to correctly implement God's will in the earth, we must operate in the authority God has given us. Just as in the days of Adam, God and man together would rule and govern the earth. This is why Psalm 8:4-6 declares that all the works of God on the earth are under man's authority.

> *What is man that You are mindful of him,*
> *And the son of man that You visit him?*
> *For You have made him a little lower than the angels,*
> *And You have crowned him with glory and honor.*

You have made him to have dominion over the works of Your hands;
You have put all things under his feet.

We have been crowned with glory and honor and given the right and privilege to rule the earth on behalf of God who sits on the Throne. Any problems in the earth are traced to our ineffectiveness and not God's. We must step up into the authority granted to us by God through the work of Jesus on the cross to restore it. When we do, we can fulfill what Jesus said we were to do in Matthew 6:9-10. We are to pray Heaven into earth so that the passion of God can be seen in this place.

In this manner, therefore, pray:
Our Father in heaven,
Hallowed be Your name.
Your kingdom come.
Your will be done
On earth as it is in heaven.

If there is not a people to pray and implement Heaven into earth, then earth becomes a place less like Heaven than God desires. However, this isn't God's fault but our failure as those set and positioned by Him. We must operate in the authority we have been granted as those set over the works of His hands and having been crowned with authority. In other words, everything we need has been provided for us.

This is why we see God declaring in Ezekiel 36:33-37 the restoration He would bring to nations.

Thus says the Lord God: "On the day that I cleanse you from all your iniquities, I will also enable you to dwell in the cities, and the ruins shall be rebuilt. The desolate land shall be tilled instead of lying desolate in the sight of all who pass by. So they will say, 'This land that was desolate has become like the garden of Eden; and the wasted, desolate, and ruined cities are now fortified and inhabited.' Then the nations which are left all around you shall know that I, the Lord, have rebuilt the ruined places and planted what was desolate. I, the Lord, have spoken it, and I will do it."

Thus says the Lord God: "I will also let the house of Israel inquire of Me to do this for them: I will increase their men like a flock."

God promises to restore and rebuild. He promises there will be a restoration of society and life in a nation that He would bless. He promises that cities will be renewed and recovered. Such great promises. Then God makes this statement: *"I will also let the house of Israel inquire of Me to do this for them."* Wow! God declares that He grants man the honor of working together with Him for His intended, promised end. The fact is, God will not accomplish His will without us taking our place in prayer for it to happen. We must *inquire of the Lord* for this to happen. Remember, prayer is not seeking to convince God to do something for us. Prayer is working together with Him to see things arranged in the spirit world, so what God longs for will occur. This is why God allows us this function and honor.

In Zechariah 12:10 we are told that God begins this process of praying that gives birth to restoration.

And I will pour on the house of David and on the inhabitants
of Jerusalem the Spirit of grace and supplication; then they
will look on Me whom they pierced. Yes, they will mourn for
Him as one mourns for his only son, and grieve for Him as
one grieves for a firstborn.

The Lord promises to pour out on us a Spirit of grace and supplication for prayer. This means that God starts the process, but
we must respond. He pours out grace and supplication, yet we
must embrace it. In other words, the impetus to pray comes from
the Lord, but I have to recognize it and move in agreement. This
is why David spoke of God speaking to him to seek His face in
Psalm 27:8 and David responding in agreement.

When You said, "Seek My face," my heart said to You,
"Your face, Lord, I will seek."

It is the Lord who stirs the heart to pray and calls us to this
place with Him. Even though it is the Lord who causes the stirring to pray, it is still our choice. David responded to the call of
God to *"Seek His face"* with a proper response to seek the face
of the Lord. God needs us to step into the realms of the Spirit
through prayer and co-laboring together with Him to birth His
desire in the earth. This is not a Sovereign God *making* us do
what He wants, however. This is the Lord giving us the opportunity and honor to move together with Him to see His passion
accomplished. If we were not to respond rightly to the persuading
of the Lord, the Lord would have to find another who would obey
Him. However, He does not *make* anyone do something outside
their free will. The purposes of God in the earth require willing

participants. Isaiah 59:1-4 shows us what happens when God doesn't cause a stirring in the heart to seek Him.

> *Behold, the Lord's hand is not shortened,*
> *That it cannot save;*
> *Nor His ear heavy,*
> *That it cannot hear.*
> *But your iniquities have separated you from your God;*
> *And your sins have hidden His face from you,*
> *So that He will not hear.*
> *For your hands are defiled with blood,*
> *And your fingers with iniquity;*
> *Your lips have spoken lies,*
> *Your tongue has muttered perversity.*
> *No one calls for justice,*
> *Nor does any plead for truth.*
> *They trust in empty words and speak lies;*
> *They conceive evil and bring forth iniquity.*

Even though the power and ability of the Lord is to deliver, they do not get the benefit of it because God has *hid His face* from them. When God hides His face, there is no stirring in the hearts of men to cry out to the Lord. In other words, as a result of the Lord not stirring the heart, they have no passion to seek Him. The consequence is that no one *calls for justice or pleads for mercy.* Only when God's face is toward us are our hearts stirred to cry out to Him. The passion and inclination to seek the face of God is a sign that God is moving us and wooing us to Himself. If we realize this, we will not neglect the longing in our heart to seek after the Lord. We will recognize it for what it is—His grace toward us. There is no nobility in and of ourselves to make us want to cry out to Him. In the midst of this, however, He is still not *making us seek Him*. We still must make the choice to come after Him and move with Him in prayer and the yearning after the Lord and His ways.

The bottom line is God must have willing participants to agree with Him for His will to be done in the earth. There is no *hyper-sovereignty of God* that forces the will of God to be done in the earth. If we are to see God's will done, it will be because we have agreed with Him for Heaven to come to earth. Should we not be willing to do this, then God will wait another generation to have a people who will. Remember that this is what He did when the people who came out of Egypt refused to go in and take the land. God had to raise another group who would believe Him and cooperate with Him. Numbers 14:26-31 shows God rejecting those who rebelled and would not go into the Promised Land. He chooses, however, the next generation.

And the Lord spoke to Moses and Aaron, saying, "How long shall I bear with this evil congregation who complain against Me? I have heard the complaints which the children of Israel make against Me. Say to them, 'As I live,' says the Lord, 'just as you have spoken in My hearing, so I will do to you: The carcasses of you who have complained against Me shall fall in this wilderness, all of you who were numbered, according to your entire number, from twenty years old and above. Except for Caleb the son of Jephunneh and Joshua the son of Nun, you shall by no means enter the land which I swore I would make you dwell in. But your little ones, whom you said would be victims, I will bring in, and they shall know the land which you have despised.'"

The result of a generation choosing to not believe the Lord was that God had to wait another 40-plus years to fulfill His purposes in a nation. He didn't just override their disobedience and impose His will. Because He needs a willing vessel and obedient servants, God had to wait to fulfill His word. This was not what the Lord would have wanted but what was necessary as a result of a stubborn people unwilling to obey. As a result of God having tied Himself to His people's obedience, sometimes God and His grace are frustrated.

The Lord must have a people who will move with Him and respond to Him for His will to be done. If we are to see a nation fulfill the will of God there must be a people who will obey and respond to God and His drawing. God needs a people who will take up His cause in the earth and agree for Heaven to bring its influence into that culture. Unless this is realized and the hyperview of God's sovereignty is forsaken, a nation and its purposes can be lost. Somehow God will accomplish His will even though at best it may require the waiting of generations. The best, however, is for there to be a people who will respond to the Lord and see God's purposes done with passion. We can secure from Heaven the future and destiny that God desires for America and the nations of the earth.

There are two essential dimensions to our partnership with God—intercession and activism. My first role before the Lord is not a minister, speaker, writer, or apostolic leader; my first role before Him is an intercessor. Thus, this book and the *Courts of Heaven* series I've written focus primarily on the intercessory aspect of this. That's the cry of my heart. In the place of prayer, however, we receive access to information and strategies in the spirit world. It's the prophetic advantage all believers have when they learn how to function in spiritual dimensions—the Counsel of the Lord, Court of Heaven, etc. Many believers operate in these places. The key is knowing where you are operating, so you can have spiritual eyes and ears open to receive intel from Heaven. This is vital, but it doesn't simply end with accessing the information.

The high-water mark of our effectiveness as the Ecclesia is not how spiritual our experiences in the heavenly realms sound, but rather how culture looks different because we are there, making the difference. In fact, I usually say the Ecclesia has two main functions. The first is to legislate in the spiritual realm everything into divine order. In other words, we must win victories in the unseen realm through prayer. The second function is to execute these victories won in the spiritual place into the natural realm. This requires *reformers*. Any victories won in the unseen dimension *not* executed into the natural realm will be forfeited. This has happened more often than we would like to admit. We as the church have secured victories from the spiritual place but we haven't seen the benefit of it for the lack of reformers. Reformers are those who not only touch things in the unseen but also are faithful in the seen realm. This can be as simple as *voting*, working in the political realm, and even running for office. It is adding our natural effort to what our spiritual activities have secured. If we don't provide natural responses to the spiritual victories that are won, nothing will ever change and in fact will only get worse.

I encourage you, as you pray for Donald J. Trump, receive assignments in the Counsel of the Lord. Listen to the prophetic voice of the Spirit leading and guiding you on how to not only pray, but participate. Go out and vote. Maybe you're called to run for a political office in the future. Maybe the Lord is directing you to be a voice of reason in the cesspool that the news media has become. Perhaps the Spirit is leading you to be a reformer in the education realm (which is undergoing significant infiltration right now by Marxist socialist ideologies). Pray and participate.

With this understood, I felt the Lord gave me another mandate to pray for the re-election of President Donald J. Trump. Just as Elijah went up the mountain and prayed after the victory on Mount Carmel against the prophets of Baal, so we are to pray. First Kings 18:41-46 shows Elijah praying into being what he was hearing in the realms of the spirit.

> Then Elijah said to Ahab, "Go up, eat and drink; for there is the sound of abundance of rain." So Ahab went up to eat and drink. And Elijah went up to the top of Carmel; then he bowed down on the ground, and put his face between his knees, and said to his servant, "Go up now, look toward the sea."
>
> So he went up and looked, and said, "There is nothing." And seven times he said, "Go again."
>
> Then it came to pass the seventh time, that he said, "There is a cloud, as small as a man's hand, rising out of the sea!" So he said, "Go up, say to Ahab, 'Prepare your chariot, and go down before the rain stops you.'"
>
> Now it happened in the meantime that the sky became black with clouds and wind, and there was a heavy rain. So Ahab rode away and went to Jezreel. Then the hand of the Lord came upon Elijah; and he girded up his loins and ran ahead of Ahab to the entrance of Jezreel.

After the fire fell on Mount Carmel, the people cried out to God, the prophets of Baal were killed, Elijah went to the top of the mountain and began to pray. He prays until the cloud the size of a man's hand appeared. It is interesting that Elijah's impetus to pray flowed from what he was hearing in the spirit realm. The sound of an abundance of rain was what Elijah was sensing. It hadn't rained for three and a half years, yet the prophet was hearing this sound. This sound is what stirred him to pray. What we hear and sense in the spirit realm is very important to partnering with God. God needed Elijah to pray into reality what God desired. If God was going to just do what He wanted anyway, why should Elijah have to pray? The answer is because God doesn't move in hyper-sovereignty. We are a necessary process of the Lord for His will to be done.

Elijah prayed until his servant saw the cloud. The small cloud turned into a black, dark sky filled with clouds, wind, and then rain. If we are to see President Trump be re-elected, there must be a people to stand before the Lord and pray until the cloud appears. We cannot take things for granted and think God will just do it. No! We must set ourselves to pray until the cloud appears, the sky becomes dark, and the rain of God begins to fall on our nations. In regard to the re-election of President Trump, I believe we must contend against voter lethargy and apathy. We must through our prayers create a stirring of God that will motivate the right people to the polls to vote. Otherwise victories that have been won can be forfeited and overturned.

Where are the Elijahs who will take their place on the mountain and pray until the cloud appears and people's hearts are stirred? Our prayer must create this stirring and birth this move that will re-elect President Donald J. Trump and reseat him as the United States president. Let the Elijahs take their place and partner with God.

Lord, as we stand before Your Courts and in Your Counsel, we repent for the times we have leaned toward a hyper-sovereignty of God viewpoint. We repent for granting ourselves license to rebel and disobey, comforting ourselves with the idea that You, Lord, would just take care of things. We repent. Lord, forgive us for spiritual laziness and neutrality. We ask, Lord, that You would not hide Your face from us but would look toward us and stir our hearts to pray and seek Your face. Create in us, Lord, a cry consistent with Your desire and passion for America and the nations of the earth. Let the cloud the size of a man's hand arise on the horizon. Allow, Lord, a stirring to occur in the hearts of the American people who would vote for President Trump. Let all voter apathy and lethargy be revoked. Cause an arising to take place that will reseat Donald J. Trump as the president of the United States of America. In Jesus' Name, amen.

Chapter 10

BOOKS OF REMEMBRANCE

WE are living in a time described in Malachi 3:15-18. In these verses we see society becoming warped and perverted away from the standards of God. We also see the Lord moving and defending His purposes in the earth. Remember that before the lamp goes out, God will move to sustain and retain His witness in the earth.

"So now we call the proud blessed,
For those who do wickedness are raised up;
They even tempt God and go free."
Then those who feared the Lord spoke to one another,
And the Lord listened and heard them;
So a book of remembrance was written before Him
For those who fear the Lord
And who meditate on His name.
"They shall be Mine," says the Lord of hosts,
"On the day that I make them My jewels.
And I will spare them
As a man spares his own son who serves him."
Then you shall again discern
Between the righteous and the wicked,
Between one who serves God
And one who does not serve Him.

Notice these verses say the proud are called blessed, the wicked are raised up, and those who tempt God go free with no results to their rebellion and sin. In other words, there seems to be no consequence to living in rebellion toward God. It would appear that they are the ones who are blessed of God. Other verses describe this as well. Isaiah 59:15 even speaks of those who would seek to walk in righteousness being punished for it.

So truth fails,
And he who departs from evil makes himself a prey.
Then the Lord saw it, and it displeased Him
That there was no justice.

Society is being described as so out of order and against God that whoever would seek to obey the Lord suffers as a result. Psalm 73:1-19 gives us further insight into this culture that would rebel toward God with seemingly no adverse results.

Truly God is good to Israel,
To such as are pure in heart.
But as for me, my feet had almost stumbled;
My steps had nearly slipped.
For I was envious of the boastful,
When I saw the prosperity of the wicked.
For there are no pangs in their death,
But their strength is firm.
They are not in trouble as other men,
Nor are they plagued like other men.
Therefore pride serves as their necklace;
Violence covers them like a garment.
Their eyes bulge with abundance;
They have more than heart could wish.
They scoff and speak wickedly concerning oppression;
They speak loftily.
They set their mouth against the heavens,
And their tongue walks through the earth.
Therefore his people return here,
And waters of a full cup are drained by them.
And they say, "How does God know?

And is there knowledge in the Most High?"
Behold, these are the ungodly,
Who are always at ease;
They increase in riches.
Surely I have cleansed my heart in vain,
And washed my hands in innocence.
For all day long I have been plagued,
And chastened every morning.
If I had said, "I will speak thus,"
Behold, I would have been untrue to the generation of Your
children.
When I thought how to understand this,
It was too painful for me—
Until I went into the sanctuary of God;
Then I understood their end.
Surely You set them in slippery places;
You cast them down to destruction.
Oh, how they are brought to desolation, as in a moment!
They are utterly consumed with terrors.

Asaph, the writer of this Psalm, is questioning his commitment to godly living in view of how it doesn't seem to pay. He declares what he is watching is actually causing him pain. He speaks of the wicked and their "blessing" that they seem to enjoy. There seems to be no restraint on the good that they experience, even though they exhibit nothing but reprehensible reproach toward God. He finishes this thought though with this conclusion. *"When I went into the sanctuary (presence) of God, I understood their end."* He then declares, *"You have set them in a slippery place. They are brought down to destruction and into desolation in a moment."* In other words, he is convinced there is justice in God.

We as believers must believe and be convinced that there will be justice from the Lord in our society. That those who flaunt themselves against God will be removed from their place and judgement that produces justice will ensue. In Malachi we see what allows this to happen. A book of remembrance is written for those who are the Lord's. This book will testify before the Lord and then allow Him the right to spare His people and judge society for its rebellion against God. Let's look at these verses again in Malachi 3:15-18.

> *"So now we call the proud blessed,*
> *For those who do wickedness are raised up;*
> *They even tempt God and go free."*
> *Then those who feared the Lord spoke to one another,*
> *And the Lord listened and heard them;*
> *So a book of remembrance was written before Him*
> *For those who fear the Lord*
> *And who meditate on His name.*
> *"They shall be Mine," says the Lord of hosts,*
> *"On the day that I make them My jewels.*
> *And I will spare them*
> *As a man spares his own son who serves him."*
> *Then you shall again discern*
> *Between the righteous and the wicked,*
> *Between one who serves God*
> *And one who does not serve Him.*

Notice that only when there is first a book of remembrance, created on behalf of those who belong to God, can God then make a distinction in culture of those who serve God and those who don't. The Lord promises to bring such judgement in righteousness into culture that again the ways of the Lord will be known. Right now, culture doesn't know the ways of God. Humanism, paganism, and new age has replaced the values of God. However, God will bring a justice into culture that will again allow people to know who He is in truth. This judgement cannot be released, however, until there is a book of remembrance written on behalf of those who belong to God. This will allow them to be spared in this day of justice. We see this pictured when God was revealing Himself to Egypt and the children of Israel were spared from the effect of the judgements. Exodus 9:25-26 shows that when judgements hit Egypt, in the land of Goshen where God's people were they were untouched.

And the hail struck throughout the whole land of Egypt, all that was in the field, both man and beast; and the hail struck every herb of the field and broke every tree of the field. Only in the land of Goshen, where the children of Israel were, there was no hail.

This and other judgements from God did not touch the people of God, because God remembered them. This is what a book of remembrance does for the people of God as God reveals Himself to nations and cultures. Ezekiel 9:4-6 shows the judgement of God coming on a culture. However, before it could come, those who cried to the Lord were marked in their forehead.

And the Lord said to him, "Go through the midst of the city, through the midst of Jerusalem, and put a mark on the fore-heads of the men who sigh and cry over all the abominations that are done within it."

To the others He said in my hearing, "Go after him through the city and kill; do not let your eye spare, nor have any pity. Utterly slay old and young men, maidens and little children and women; but do not come near anyone on whom is the mark; and begin at My sanctuary." So they began with the elders who were before the temple.

Those who cried and lamented over the abominations and sin within the culture were sealed and spared. They had to be marked before God could bring judgement into the situation. This is always the process of God. This is why Malachi is declaring that judgement can only begin *after* a book of remembrance is written to cause God to recognize and remember those who are His. This is what is hindering and delaying the Lord causing it to be known who belongs to Him and who doesn't.

There are three things Malachi speaks of that allow a book of remembrance to be written that causes God to remember His people. When this happens, God is now free to allow Himself to be known and to arise in zeal and reclaim a culture. First of all, we are told that those who *fear the Lord* will have a book of remembrance written on their behalf. Fearing the Lord is a realization that not only is God merciful, but He is also holy. When we know that God is holy and requires that of us as well, it births the fear of God in us. Second Corinthians 7:1 tells us that we are to perfect holiness in the fear of the Lord.

Therefore, having these promises, beloved, let us cleanse ourselves from all filthiness of the flesh and spirit, perfecting holiness in the fear of God.

When we fear the Lord, we are aware of the holiness of His nature. We will have a cry in our hearts for holiness that is created by the Holy Spirit as a result of having received the nature of God Himself. It is impossible to live in sin and not be miserable when God's divine nature is in us. We received this nature at our salvation. Second Peter 1:4 declares that as a result of this divine nature we now long for holy and godly things.

> By which have been given to us exceedingly great and precious promises, that through these you may be partakers of the divine nature, having escaped the corruption that is in the world through lust.

As a result of the divine nature of God in us, we are empowered to escape the corruption in the world from lust. We are no longer ruled by a lustful nature but God's nature in us. When this nature is in us, there is a cry for holiness that is driven by the fear of the Lord. We long to please Him and be holy and pure before Him.

The second thing that will cause the book of remembrance to be written is *they spoke often one to each other*. This speaks of fellowship and not forsaking the assembling of ourselves together. Hebrews 10:25 exhorts us to come together in fellowship and to exhort each other.

> Not forsaking the assembling of ourselves together, as is the manner of some, but exhorting one another, and so much the more as you see the Day approaching.

These would seem like such simple things that would cause a book of remembrance to be written that would cause God to remember us and spare us. Yet these things obviously impress the Lord. We are to come together as the people of God in fellowship and communion. We are to share with each other the goodness of the Lord. Heaven records these activities. The word *forsaking* in the Greek is the word *egkataleipo*. It means to *leave behind*. We are not to *leave behind* our fellowship with each other. We are not to get so busy that we exclude this necessary part of being a believer. Not only does this bring strength and keep us encouraged, it is recorded in Heaven and acknowledged there. This is part of what causes a book of remembrance to be written.

The third thing is they *meditated on His Name*. This is the idea of pondering until we gain deeper understanding of the Lord and His ways. If our mind is actively involved in meditating on the Lord, we will come to greater and new revelations of Him. Joshua 1:8 tells us to *meditate* on the Word and the law of the Lord.

> *This Book of the Law shall not depart from your mouth, but you shall meditate in it day and night, that you may observe to do according to all that is written in it. For then you will make your way prosperous, and then you will have good success.*

Notice that as we meditate our way will become prosperous and we will have good success. Meditating allows a renewing of the mind that we begin to think according to the ways of the Lord. In Ephesians 4:22-23 we are told to be renewed in the spirit of our minds.

That you put off, concerning your former conduct, the old man which grows corrupt according to the deceitful lusts, and be renewed in the spirit of your mind.

As our meditation renews our mind, we are able to separate ourselves from the old activities of the flesh. We are empowered to walk in a holy way before the Lord. The Hebrew word for *meditate* is *hagah*. It means to murmur. In other words, we are to speak to ourselves the Word of God. So often we are guilty of murmuring negatively. We are told we should *murmur* the Word of the Lord to ourselves. As we do, we are meditating on His Name. The result is new realms of revelation are unlocked but also books of remembrance are written about us in Heaven.

Once this is in place, God is now ready to judge the earth and bring cultures to justice. He will be able to manifest those who are His and those who are not. There will be a shifting from the proud being called blessed to the humble being revered and applauded. Instead of the wicked being touted, the godly will be renowned. Instead of those who tempt God going free, the righteous will be the delivered ones. The culture will shift because those who belong to God have done the necessary things for a book of remembrance to be written about them. God is now able to render judgement and justice because His people are walking in obedience before Him. We are not waiting on the Lord for judgement. The Lord is waiting on us to step into divine order that His judgements might come into our culture. Lord, help us that a book of remembrance might be written in Heaven and speak before You concerning us!

Lord, as we stand before Your Courts and in Your Counsel, we repent for not walking in the fear of the Lord. We repent for not speaking often one to each other and for forsaking the assembling of ourselves before You. We also repent for not meditating on Your Name. Lord, we recognize that You cannot judge and bring justice to our culture until a book of remembrance is written about Your people. We ask, Lord, that You would forgive us. Let us obey Your Word and allow this book of remembrance to be recorded concerning us. Lord, let it be known the difference between those who serve You and those who do not, that the ways of the Lord might be known in America and the nations of the earth. In Jesus' Name, amen!

Chapter 11

A CRY FOR MERCY

IN the midst of our contending for the destiny and future of America and the nations, we must present our case in the Courts and before the Counsel of the Lord. As in the election in November 2016, I believe one of our chief cries must be for mercy. Mercy is a verdict that can be rendered from the Court of Heaven. We cannot stand before the Court of Heaven as a nation and ask for justice on the basis of our righteousness. There is not enough sufficiency of righteousness for this. It is very much as in the days when the children of Israel were in Babylonian captivity, yet the time for deliverance had come. Their prayer was based on the mercy of God's character and not on their own righteousness. Daniel 9:18 shows Daniel crying out on the basis of God's mercies.

> O my God, incline Your ear and hear; open Your eyes and see our desolations, and the city which is called by Your name; for we do not present our supplications before You because of our righteous deeds, but because of Your great mercies.

Notice that the cry for the deliverance of a nation was on the basis of God's great mercies and not their righteous deeds. Ultimately, this is what we must do as a nation. During the 2016 election cycle, we were told by the Lord to cry for mercy as we contended for Donald Trump to be elected. We do not want what we deserve. We need the mercy of God concerning our nation and its election. We must ask again in this cycle for God to again have mercy of us. James 2:12-13 tells us that mercy will speak for us if we have been merciful.

So speak and so do as those who will be judged by the law of liberty. For judgment is without mercy to the one who has shown no mercy. Mercy triumphs over judgment.

We are judged by the law of liberty. We are told that if we have shown mercy, we will be given mercy. Mercy will triumph and win out over every call for judgement in the Courts of Heaven before our judge. As a nation we must repent for every place we haven't been merciful. However, it is appropriate to bring before the Court of Heaven the places we have shown mercy even to other nations. We so often think of and repent for the grievous sins of our past and history as a nation. However, we can also *humbly* present before the Lord the places we might have been merciful and kind to other nations. We do have this in the history of America as well. We can ask the Lord for mercy in this election on the basis of His mercy, but also recalling before Him our places of showing mercy. We can ask again that the Lord would be kind and reseat President Donald J. Trump as our president.

To fully embrace this idea, we must know that God is merciful in His person. He is always looking for a right to show mercy. Second Samuel 14:14 shows a woman speaking to King David and exhorting him to bring his estranged son home.

For we will surely die and become like water spilled on the ground, which cannot be gathered up again. Yet God does not take away a life; but He devises means, so that His banished ones are not expelled from Him.

God does not take away life but devises and considers ways to bring ones expelled from Him home. The Lord loves mercy and desires reconciliation. He is not looking for the reason to condemn but to save. John 3:17 clearly states this idea.

> *For God did not send His Son into the world to condemn the world, but that the world through Him might be saved.*

The reason for Jesus coming was to save the world, not condemn it. God's passion is to manifest His kindness and goodness from generation to generation and even age to age. The devil would approach the Court of Heaven and seek to make a case for destruction and loss of future over America and the nations. However, if we as God's people can cry out for His mercy and present a case before God concerning this, we can see this secured. America will be saved. We will see the purpose of God done. Not because we deserve it, but because of His great mercies toward us.

As we approach the time of the elections in 2020, we must stand before the Courts of Heaven and contend for the mercies of God. We are granted the privilege of presenting cases before His Courts that will allow God to shine His merciful face on our nations again. Micah 7:18-20 gives us a resounding statement to build our faith as we cry for mercy from the Courts of Heaven.

> *Who is a God like You,*
> *Pardoning iniquity*
> *And passing over the transgression of the remnant of His heritage?*
> *He does not retain His anger forever,*
> *Because He delights in mercy.*
> *He will again have compassion on us,*
> *And will subdue our iniquities.*

You will cast all our sins
Into the depths of the sea.
You will give truth to Jacob
And mercy to Abraham,
Which You have sworn to our fathers
From days of old.

On the basis of this precious promise may we petition the Lord for His mercies for America and the nations of the earth.

Lord, as we stand before Your Courts we declare, "Who is like You?" You, Lord, pardon iniquity, and You, Lord, pass over transgression. Lord, we acknowledge we are guilty. However, Lord, You also delight in mercy. We ask that You would again have compassion on America and the nations. Subdue all our iniquities and sins and don't allow them to speak against us. We ask for Your blood, Lord Jesus, to speak for us and our nations (Heb. 12:24). We ask, Lord, that You would remember the covenant with our fathers that we have with You. Lord, You have birthed America. Please, Lord, do not forsake or cast us away. In the midst of our evil, wickedness, and transgressions, would You also remember the places we as a nation have shown mercy to others. We have not always been righteous. However, we have demonstrated Your kindness in our history. Please, Lord, do not forget or dismiss this.

We ask, Lord, that a verdict and decision would be rendered from Your Court to re-elect President Donald J. Trump. Allow, Lord, Your purposes to be fulfilled through him and in him. Arise, Lord, and contend against all that contend against him and perform Your will through Him to recover America and the nations to their destiny. In Jesus' Name, amen!

ROBERT HENDERSON is a global, apostolic leader who operates in revelation and impartation. His teaching empowers the body of Christ to see the hidden truths of Scripture clearly and apply them for breakthrough results. Driven by a mandate to disciple nations through writing and speaking, Robert travels extensively around the globe, teaching on the apostolic, the Kingdom of God, the "Seven Mountains," and most notably, the Courts of Heaven. He has been married to Mary for 40 years. They have six children and five grandchildren. Together they are enjoying life in beautiful Midlothian, Texas.